W. H Wylie

The Book of the Bunyan Festival

A Complete Record of the Proceedings at the Unveiling of the Statue given

by his Grace, the Duke of Bedford, June 10, 1874

W. H Wylie

The Book of the Bunyan Festival
A Complete Record of the Proceedings at the Unveiling of the Statue given by his Grace, the Duke of Bedford, June 10, 1874

ISBN/EAN: 9783337093112

Printed in Europe, USA, Canada, Australia, Japan

Cover: Foto ©ninafisch / pixelio.de

More available books at **www.hansebooks.com**

THE BOOK

OF

THE BUNYAN FESTIVAL.

A COMPLETE RECORD

OF THE PROCEEDINGS AT

THE UNVEILING OF THE STATUE

GIVEN BY

HIS GRACE THE DUKE OF BEDFORD,

JUNE 10, 1874.

Revised and Published by Authority.

EDITED BY W. H. WYLIE.

WITH

AN HISTORICAL SKETCH BY THE REV. J. BROWN, B.A.,
Of Bunyan Meeting, Bedford.

London:
JAMES CLARKE & CO., "CHRISTIAN WORLD" OFFICE,
13, FLEET STREET, E.C.
ROWLAND HILL & SONS, "MERCURY" OFFICE, HIGH STREET, BEDFORD.

1874.

TO

ALDERMAN GEORGE HURST,

MAYOR OF BEDFORD,

AND THE

MEMBERS OF THE CORPORATION,

This Memorial Volume

IS

BY THEIR SPECIAL PERMISSION

RESPECTFULLY DEDICATED.

CONTENTS.

	PAGE
AN HISTORICAL SKETCH. *By the Rev. J. Brown, B.A.*	1
THE FESTIVAL AT BEDFORD, JUNE 10, 1874. *By the Editor.*	22
Preparatory Sermons	24
Relics of Bunyan	26
The Procession to the Statue	27
The Unveiling of the Statue	29
The Statue	31
Meeting in the Exchange	33
Open-air Meetings	37
Treat to the Children	39
Lecture by Rev. C. M. Birrell	40
The Hospitalities of the Day	41
THE PRISONER OF BEDFORD. *By Alderman George Hurst, Mayor of Bedford*	43
THE CHARACTER OF JOHN BUNYAN. *By the Very Rev. A. P. Stanley, D.D., Dean of Westminster*	46
DEAN STANLEY, THE CHURCH, AND BUNYAN. *By the Right Hon. Earl Cowper, K.G., Lord-Lieutenant of Bedfordshire*	56
BUNYAN AND RELIGIOUS LIBERTY. *By the Rev. W. Brock, D.D.*	59
THE LITERARY GENIUS OF JOHN BUNYAN. *By the Rev. Henry Allon, D.D.*	65

Contents.

	PAGE
THE STATUE AND THE TIME. *By the Rev. J. Brown, B.A.*	75
BUNYAN'S PERSONAL PILGRIMAGE. *By the Rev. C. M. Birrell*	79
THE SCENERY AND CHARACTERS OF BUNYAN. *By the Rev. J. Stoughton, D.D.*	109
THE SECRET OF BUNYAN'S INFLUENCE. *By S. Whitbread, Esq., M.P.*	111
THE NEWSPAPER PRESS ON THE CELEBRATION	113
The Paralysed Demon of Intolerance.—*The Times*	113
Bunyan's Bedford Life.—*Daily News*	113
Vanity Fair and the Pilgrim.—*Daily Telegraph*	114
A Tory Counterblast.—*The Standard*	115
The "Pilgrim's" Chief Service to Mankind.—*The Echo*	115
The Victory of Genius.—*The Spectator*	116
Bunyan at Bedford.—*Punch*	116
"The Whirligig of Time."—*English Independent*	118
The Triumph of Christian Charity.—"*An Eye-witness*" in the *Freeman*	118
Popish and Clerical Slander against Bunyan	119

THE BOOK

OF THE

BUNYAN FESTIVAL.

An Historical Sketch.

BY THE REV. JOHN BROWN, B.A.
Of Bunyan Meeting.

HAVING been asked to write a preface to this Memorial volume, it occurs to me that I can best keep clear of the various lines of thought pursued by others, and add to the general interest, by a little historical sketch which shall give the old story in the light of some recent researches, and with some little additions which circumstances have placed within my reach.

The name of Bunyan as a surname of the living has almost died out from Bunyan's native county. I only remember to have met with it once or twice. Yet it is of considerable antiquity, and was at one time far from rare. A document now being edited by H. Gough, Esq., shows that one William Boynyon, of Stanbridge, in Leighton Buzzard, was a member of a guild or fraternity at Luton, in 1518. The name is found variously spelt. In the Church Registers of Elstow and Wootton, it is written thus, Bannion or Banion. In the original accounts of the real and personal estates of delinquents seized by the Parliament of England, between the years 1642 and 1648, the rent of Sir George Bynnion, delinquent, in the parish of Eaton Socon, Bedfordshire, is returned at £223 11s. 4d.* From the same account it appears that the land of Mr. Foster, delinquent, in the parish of Stretly, was let by the year to John Bunnyon, tenant, at a rent of £30. It is, perhaps, worthy of notice, that the farm of this John Bunnyon, was not far from that village of Samsell where our John Bunyan was apprehended for preaching. Were they kinsmen, and had the tinker been on a visit to his more prosperous relative when he fell into trouble? Quite recently also it has been discovered that between October, 1581, and January, 1645, the name Bunnion or Bunion occurs no less than sixteen times in the Register of the Parish Church at Wootton, a village some three or four miles from Elstow. There can be little doubt that these different modes of spelling are simply variations of the same name, and their long existence in the county effectually disposes of the groundless supposition that the Bunyans were gypsies.

Mr. Blower, of Bedford, who has long taken deep interest in all that belongs to Bunyan, maintains that it is not strictly correct to say that he was born in Elstow parish. The tradition held many years ago by the oldest inhabitants was that the cottage where he was born stood in a field a little way over the parish boundary in the hamlet of Harrowden and parish of Cardington. The cottage has long been pulled down, and the field ploughed up, but the place is still called Bunyan's End, and a part of a neighbouring farm used to be pointed out as Bunyan's Walk. But whether this tradition be true or not, Bunyan's personal relations with Elstow parish were of the closest kind. It was in Elstow Church that he looked up with reverential awe to Christopher Hall, the Puritan preacher, who held the living in the Commonwealth days; it was in the tower, perhaps once united to the Church by the Conventual

---

* Additional MSS., 5,494.

buildings, but now standing separate, that he rang the bells and was harassed by his fears and misgivings; it was in the old Moot Hall on the Green that he is said to have danced with the Elstow lasses, an exercise so much to his mind, that, as he says, "it was a full year before I could quite leave that;" it was on the Green itself, which to this day lies so charmingly in the summer sunlight, that he joined in the village sports and heard those inward voices which filled his soul with the terrors of the unseen; and there can be no doubt it was to the unpretending cottage by the roadside as you enter Elstow that he brought home his bride. There it was that the young people started life together with large faith, kindling hope, and clinging love, with "these three, faith, hope, and love," but with not much else, for, says he, "we came together as poor as poor might be, not having so much household stuff as a dish or a spoon betwixt us both."

But before his marriage, and during his Elstow days, Bunyan's soldiering experiences came in. On which side in the civil wars he took up arms is still a moot point. His most recent biographers, Mr. Offor and Mr. Copner, are both of them strongly of opinion that he was a Royalist, the latter gentleman holding that there is "not a tittle of evidence" in favour of his being on the side of the Parliament. For my own part, I have been led to a different conclusion. It is true that, some fifteen years after the first civil war came to an end, Bunyan speaks with loyalty of the then reigning King. When Cobb, the Clerk of the Peace, came to him in prison, Bunyan repudiated the conduct of those who had just raised the Venner insurrection in London, and of all who met for political purposes, under cover of religious exercises, and said, "I look upon it as my duty to behave myself under the King's Government both as becomes a man and a Christian, and if the occasion were offered me, I should willingly manifest my loyalty to my Prince both by word and deed."

It would greatly have strengthened his words if he could have added that, in byegone years, he had taken up arms for the King's father. He does not say this when he might have said it to purpose, and all that his words can be made to mean is that he was no plotter at the meetings to which he gathered the people, but that he was a law-abiding, peaceable man, and ready to prove his loyalty to lawfully-constituted authority. But at the time when Bunyan was a soldier, it was a disputed question which was the lawfully-constituted authority of the realm—King or Parliament; and Bedfordshire gave its verdict most unmistakably for the Parliament, and against the King. It is true that Sir Lewis Dyves, of Bromham, fought as a Royalist, and once made a raid upon the town of Bedford, with brief success; several of the gentry of the county also sympathised with the King, as is shown by the lists of those who compounded for their estates at Goldsmiths' Hall. But the majority of the inhabitants were strongly Puritan. In 1634, Archbishop Laud reports to the King that his visitors "found Bedfordshire most tainted of any part of the diocese" of Lincoln; and when the great struggle began, within four months of the day on which the Royal Standard was raised at Nottingham, there was exhibited in the market-places of Bedford and Cambridge "A Remonstrance and Petition," announcing that the inhabitants of these two counties, with those of Bucks and Herts, had associated themselves and taken up arms, and did "solemnly protest and covenant before God, and with one another, that they will willingly and resolutely sacrifice their lives in this religious and just quarrel, and will never lay down their arms till this, which is called the King's army, be dissolved." To this strenuous resolution Bedfordshire was certainly true, till Bunyan's soldiering days were over. Therefore, if, at the age of sixteen or seventeen, he may be supposed to have had strong Royalist convictions, the difficulty of his carrying them into effect practically was enormous. For all along the north, the west, and south-west, Bedfordshire was shut in by one of the strongest lines of defence which the Parliamentary forces possessed. Newport Pagnell, being "geometrically situated" between the associated counties and the Royalist operations in the west, was held as of first importance. It was early seized by Sir Lewis Dyves for the King, but was recaptured for the Parliament, November, 1643. The following month, an ordinance of Parliament states "that the Lords and Commons, taking into their serious consideration the great importance of the town of Newport Pagnel, in the county of Bucks, to the safety of the country adjacent, and of all the associated counties under the command of the Earl of Essex, do ordain and order that the said town shall be strongly fortified, and furnished for garrison." This garrison was placed under the command of Sir Samuel Luke, of Cople, as Governor, and for the next three years it was a powerful base of operations for the safe keeping of Bedfordshire and the parts adjacent. Thus, then, the case against the probability of Bunyan's being in the Royal army at the siege of Leicester is this: First, it is not likely that he, a mere lad of sixteen or seventeen, listening to a Puritan preacher, and living in a county intensely Puritan, should have come to different conclusions from the majority of his neighbours on the great question then agitating the nation. Next, even if this were the case, it is very improbable that he would be able to make his way to the King's quarters through strong lines of Parliament forces, and along roads jealously guarded. And, finally, the fact has been overlooked that the King did not move upon Leicester from the south, but from the north. On the 26th of May, 1645, he marched from Stone, in Staffordshire, to Ashby, and from Ashby to Leicester, which he besieged on the 31st. Looking at all the facts of the case as far as we know them, it seems to me more than probable that Bunyan's soldiering experiences were in the service of the Parliament, and confined to the garrison of Newport Pagnel; for there is positive evidence that the villages of Bedfordshire had to furnish levies of men as soldiers for the garrison and labourers for the fortifications. The Parliamentary Ordinance, already quoted, provides "That the county of Bedford within fourteen days shall send into the said garrison 225 able and armed men for souldiers." Sir Samuel Luke's Letter Book, during the years he was Governor of Newport, extends to three volumes, and is still preserved.[*] From this we learn that the levies were very systematically made from every hundred in the county, and that as late as April, 1645, "prest men" were sent in from Bedfordshire to Newport. Some letters show that exemption was very difficult to obtain. Under date March 17, 1644, there is an earnest entreaty from William Dell, the Rector of Yelden, that John Gell, of his parish, "a man which hath a family, and is engaged in service," may be excused; and one Paul Godfrey, "a lusty fellow that hath neither wife nor child, nor any certain employment, may be ordered in his roome." I suspect that John Bunyan, answering very much to the description of Paul Godfrey, found his way to Newport Garrison, with very little choice in the matter, and for some months, at least, took part in the scenes enacted there.

The only reference Bunyan himself makes to his military experiences is the well-known passage: "When I was a soldier, I, with others, were drawn out to go to such a place to besiege it; but when I was just ready to go, one of the company desired to go in my room, to which, when I had consented, he took my place, and coming to the siege, as he stood sentinel, he was shot into the head with a musket bullet, and died." This is the passage which has been supposed to refer to the siege of Leicester. It more probably refers to some sudden call made upon the garrison

[*] Egerton MSS., 785-6-7.

at Newport for men to assist in the Parliamentary operations in the west. But wherever it was, it is clear that Bunyan did not go to the siege referred to, for he says that a substitute offered himself and went in his place. And it is somewhat curious that with his own words before them most of his biographers give graphic descriptions of a siege, as if Bunyan were present when he so plainly says he was not; and a recent illustration of the "Grace Abounding" depicts him in the attitude of contemplating the dead body of his comrade—a thing which must have been very difficult to do, seeing that he was certainly many miles away at the time the man was shot.

To pass now to other matters: Bunyan has told us himself as only he could, how he went through spiritual stress and storm, and how he came to find help and home in the little Church at Bedford which had Gifford for its pastor. It was only a year or two before his joining it that the Church had been formed by twelve brethren and sisters banding themselves together. As among these twelve were the three or four poor women whom Bunyan saw sitting at a door in the sun, and overheard talking of the higher life, "as if joy did make them speak," it may be well to give their names to a wider circle. They were: "Mr. John Grew and his wife, Mr. John Eston and his wife, Anthony Harrington and his wife, Mr. John Gifford, Sister Coventon, Sister Bosworth, Sister Munnes, Sister Fenne, and Sister Norton, and Sister Spencer, all ancient and grave Christians, well-knowne one to another, Sister Norton being the youngest." Bunyan's name is the 19th in the list of members, but as the acts of the Church are not recorded till 1656, or six years after its formation, we have no account of his reception among them besides that which he gives himself. The first mention of him beyond the record of his name is in 1657, and there are about a dozen references to him from this date to the time of his imprisonment in 1660. An entry in the autumn of 1657 shows that by that time he had become an important member of the brotherhood. It runs as follows:—" Whereas there hath heretofore been time spent in seeking God to direct us in choyce of officers necessary for ye congregation, according to the order of the Gospell; and whereas heretofore there were nominated and appointed for tryall our bro. Spencely, bro. Bunyan, bro. Coventon, and bro. Wallis, to exercise the office of Deacons; and bro. Bunyan being taken off by the preaching of the Gospell; We are agreed That bro. Bunyan being otherwise imployed: our other three brethren before-named be continued." John Fenne was added in Bunyan's place.

It was not long, however, before his zeal brought trouble upon himself and anxiety upon his brethren. On the 25th March, 1658, "It was agreed that the 3rd day of the next month be set apart to seeke God in the behalf of the Church affaires, and the affaires of the nation, and for our bro. Whitbread, who hath bene long ill: and also for counsaile what to doe with respect to the indictment against bro. Bunyan at ye Assizes for preaching at Eaton." This was in the Presbyterian days of the Commonwealth. Clearly the tinker's preaching orders were irregular in the eyes of presbyter as well as priest. Religious liberty had not yet come to mean liberty all round, but only liberty for a certain recognised section. The Quakers of Bedfordshire found that out as well as Bunyan; for, as Besse tells us, a year or two before, Isabel Parlour was sent to Bridewell for a month, with an order to be whipt, for exhorting the people in Ampthill Market to repentance and amendment of life. The same year "the Priest of Risely" caused three men and two women to be set in the stocks for three hours because in meeting with him they had "reproved him in a Scriptural manner." No doubt they were very provoking, but one would have thought this would have been sufficient without following it up the next Quarter Sessions by sending them to Bridewell for a month. About the same time also two other Quakers, "John Impey, of Barton, and his wife, were imprisoned three months for having taken each other in marriage otherwise than in the form appointed by the Directory." How Bunyan came to escape we have no means of knowing now. That he did escape seems certain, as we hear no more of the indictment at the Assizes, and he himself makes no reference to any imprisonment previous to 1660.

The last entry in the church book referring to Bunyan before his imprisonment is in the early part of 1660, and is to this effect: "It was ordered according to our agreement that our bro. Bunyan do prepare to speake a word to us the next Church meeting, and that our bro. Whiteman fail not to speake to him of it." Let us hope brother Whiteman did not fail, for the opportunities of hearing brother Bunyan will be but few for some years to come. The time they have fixed for him "to speake a word" is the time which destiny has fixed for King Charles to make that landing at Dover which will bring many changes to them and to others.

Bunyan was one of the very first to feel the ill effects of the Restoration, for under an unrepealed Act of Parliament [35 Eliz., c. i.], and within six months of the King's arrival, he was arrested for preaching at Samsell by Harlington. The chamber in which he appeared before the neighbouring justice, Francis Wingate, is still preserved very much as it was then. Wingate tried remonstrance first, but finding that unavailing he sent his prisoner on to Bedford Gaol. It is most probable that Bunyan would have to walk the thirteen miles which lay between Harlington and Bedford, and if he went along the most obvious road which is marked on an old country map of that time, after travelling through the beautiful surroundings of Silsoe on to Clophill and Wilshamstead, he would have to walk through Elstow in the custody of the constable—an event which we may be sure created no small stir among his old neighbours. Past the cottage door where he had lived with her who was now in heaven; past the old green and the ploughed fields associated with his spiritual struggles, along the road where he had once thought of putting his faith to the test of miracle, and where God was now putting it to a nobler test than that, he makes his way on to Bedford and over Bedford Bridge, constable and he still walking together, till at last they come to the grim structure of the county gaol, at the corner of what is now the Silver Street. They quickly pass within, and as the old gate swings heavily behind them it shuts some pleasant things out from him, but it shuts in with him a divine compensation, for it is of this very journey he speaks when he says, "Blessed be the Lord, I went away to prison with God's comfort in my poor soul."

After he had lain there some seven weeks, the Quarter Sessions came on, and in a document into which the lawyers had put more than their usual professional heartiness, Bunyan was indicted "for devilishly and perniciously abstaining from coming to church." He has immortalised the country gentlemen who that day acted as Justices of the Peace. John Kelynge, who lived somewhere between Shefford and Southill, was Chairman of the Sessions. He had been trained for the bar, and a few weeks before Bunyan's trial he had acted as junior counsel for the Crown in the trial of the regicides. Two years later he conducted the prosecution of Sir Harry Vane. His zeal so commended him to the ruling party that he rose rapidly in his profession, and in brief space became Lord Chief Justice. The report of Bunyan's trial shows that Kelynge was a violent man. He once fined a jury one hundred marks each because they acquitted a few poor people who met one Sunday with Bibles without Prayer Books. He had the reputation of being more fit to charge Roundheads under Prince Rupert than to charge juries from the bench of justice. But, like men of his bullying sort, he could be cowardly enough if danger threatened himself. His arbitrary proceedings and contemptuous allusions to Magna Charta once brought him under the notice of Parliament, and he escaped the consequences of his conduct only by an act of the most obsequious submission. At Bunyan's trial, of course, he simply acted as a county magistrate. The next year he was knighted, and became M.P. for Bedford. By his first wife, the daughter of Sir Thomas Boteler, of Biddenham, he was the father of Sir John Kelynge, of Southill. His course, as will be seen, was rapidly prosperous, but it was soon run, for before Bunyan was released from prison, this man had gone to his great account. The other justices at Bunyan's trial were Sir Henry Chester, of Beckring's Park, Lidlington; Sir George Blundell, of Cardington; Sir William Beecher, of Howbury Hall, Renhold; and Thomas Snagg, of Millbrook, afterwards High Sheriff. Of these gentlemen we only know that Sir Henry Chester did what he could in the Swan Chamber to silence the appeal which Bunyan's noble wife made to Sir Matthew Hale on her husband's behalf, and that Sir George Blundell was, some years afterwards, still actively engaged in persecuting the Nonconformists of Bedfordshire. When their property had been distrained and put up for sale, on one occasion nobody would buy, and Sir George exclaimed angrily that "he would sell a cow for a shilling, rather than the work should not go forward." These were the men before whom Bunyan had to answer for preaching at Samsell. There could be but one result. He was had "home to prison," there to tarry, with perhaps a brief interval in 1666, for twelve long years.

His confinement was not very rigorous at first. During 1661 he was occasionally at the Church Meetings, as the Church Book shows. There is the following entry:— "Our meetings of this sort" (*i.e.*, for business as distinguished from worship) "having been for some time neglected through the increase of trouble, the 28th of the 6th month (1661) the Church, through mercy, againe met. Agreed," among other things, that " our bro. Bunyan be sent to Robert Nelson and Sister Manley." The next month we find this—" We desire bro. Bunyan and bro. John Fenne to go again to Sister Pecock, of Okely." This comparative liberty was, however, but of brief duration. The next seven years were years of deep darkness and trouble, and during all that time Bunyan's name is not even mentioned in the Records. The Records themselves are very scanty till 1668. For four years and a half after the passing of the Conventicle Act there is a gap without a single entry. Then, after this long interval, "on the 30th day of the 8th month, 1668, it is agreed that bro. Bunyan should speake with bro. Robt. Nelson, and admonish him for withdrawing from the Church, and other miscarriages. It was desired also that bro. Bunyan and bro. Harrington send for bro. Merrill, and admonish him concerning his withdrawing from the Church, and his conformity to the world's way of worship." Eleven months later, and again two months after that, Bunyan was sent to this backsliding brother with fresh admonition, which, however, seems to have been to little purpose, for a short time afterwards Humphrey Merrill " openly recanted his profession at a General Quarter Sessions."

From 1668 till his release in 1672, Bunyan is frequently mentioned in the records of the Church. That he had some measure of liberty during five years out of the twelve is tolerably clear, though whether the story of his going abroad and coming back of his own accord in time to save the gaoler and himself is true or not, is not so clear. It is somewhat remarkable that a precisely similar story is told by John Gratton, a Quaker, of himself. In 1683 he was confined in Derby gaol, and he relates how the gaoler gave him leave to go home sometimes, his home being at a distance from Derby. On one occasion an exercise fell upon him, and he returned sooner than the gaoler expected. He goes on to say: "When I had been a little time at the gaol, there came two high priests and one called a gentleman with them to see me and asked for me, so I came to them, but when they saw me they had nothing to say to me; when they were gone the gaoler rejoiced greatly and said he would not for £40 but that I had been there that day, for one of the priests was the chief priest of Derby town and the other was very high; and he was so pleased that he let me go home again the same day." Is it possible that the similar story about Bunyan sprang out of this, for Bunyan does not relate the story himself?

But though his confinement was somewhat relaxed it was irksome enough, we may be sure. A man of the name of John Bubb, from Leighton Buzzard, who was in Bedford gaol along with Bunyan, and who was there only about nine months of 1665-6, sent a most plaintive petition to the King, saying, that during his imprisonment he "hath suffered as much misery as soe dismall a place could be capable to inflict, and so is likely to perish without Your Majestie's farther compassion and mercy towards him."* In a petition which he also sent to Sir William Morton, one of the Judges of Assize at Bedford, he desires to be "released from prison where he hath long remained in a calamitous condicon." John Bubb was clearly not of the mind of those who make light of Bunyan's twelve years' imprisonment in Bedford gaol because it had some mitigations, but then John Bubb spoke from nine months' experience, and these gentlemen do not. It may be worth while to mention by the way, that this man was ultimately released on the testimony "of a *gentlewoman surgeon* of good repute." Dorothy Sparkes, *surgeon*, of Woburn, testified that the man whom Bubb was said to have killed lived a month after the blow he received, and really died from another cause.

---

* State Papers. Domestic. Chas. II., Vol. cxcii., 33.

Unfortunately this "gentlewoman surgeon" was not able to help Bunyan as she had helped his fellow-prisoner. She was not able to certify that nobody was really the worse for Bunyan's preaching, so he had to tarry on for six years more in "calamitous condicon." But his turn, too, came at last. It has been repeatedly affirmed that his release was brought about through the kind offices of Dr. Barlow, Bishop of Lincoln. Bishops in those days did so many things of which we are sorry to hear, that one would have been glad to be able to place this humane act to the credit of my Lord of Lincoln. But I am afraid truth forbids. During the greater part of his Episcopal life he was a near neighbour of Bunyan's it is true, for he loved his palace between Kimbolton and Huntingdon more than his Cathedral, and is described as "the Bishop of Bugden that never saw Lincoln." But he was certainly not the means of Bunyan's release, for Bunyan was out of prison three years before Barlow was made Bishop at all. On his subsequent Episcopal visitations at Bedford, he may have been kind to the Nonconformist preacher in the orchard in Mill Lane, but even that I fear is doubtful. It is true that in 1660 Dr. Barlow wrote to Sir Robert Boyle in favour of toleration, but in 1679 he had changed his views, for in that year he published a treatise on the canon law for whipping heretics, with evident approval of the said law. And in 1684 he published a charge to his clergy, calling upon them to enforce the laws against the Dissenters, "agreeably to the resolution of the Bedfordshire Justices adopted at Ampthill" on the previous 14th of January. In this charge he both justifies and enforces the persecution of Dissenters as necessary to "bring them to a sense of their duty by the blessing of God for that *afflictio dat intellectum.*" In fact, a little more "*afflictio*" in Bedford gaol might have even brought Bunyan's "*intellectus*" up to that standard of "robust mediocrity" which is said to be of the essence of a Bishop. Poor Dr. Barlow!

Soon after the Toleration Act came in, he went on his way, and men saw him no more.

The documents which Mr. Offor so patiently brought to light show that the Quakers had a good deal to do with Bunyan's release, but also, I think, it came about largely because in that same year, 1672, there was a lull in the storm which had now lasted for twelve years. Possibly from some momentary weariness in the cruel work of suppression, "seeing that there is so little fruit of all these forcible courses," or more probably from a policy meant to favour Rome, the prison doors were thrown open. A Declaration of Indulgence was issued, under which more than 3,000 licences to preach were granted, and Bunyan's was one of the first.

The little Church meeting in that barn in the orchard in Mill Lane felt the approach of relief. "A meeting was held at Bedford on the 6th day of the tenth moneth to pray and consult about the choyce of bro. Bunyan to office, and a general meeting was summoned for the 21st of the same month." This last was a great meeting indeed, as the following record shows: "At a full assembly of the Church at Bedford, the 21st of the 10th moneth; [January, 1672;] after much seeking God by prayer and sober conference formerly had, the congregation did at this meeting with joynt consent (signified by the solemn lifting up of their hands) call forth and appoint our bro. John Bunyan to the pastoral office or eldership; and he accepting thereof, gave up himself to serve Christ and His Church in that charge, and received of the elders the right hand of fellowship."

It was a Pentecostal season, indeed, for at the same time the tongue of fire seemed to rest on many heads. The record goes on to say, "The same time, and after the same manner, the Church did solemnly approve the gifts of (and called to the work of the ministry) these brethren: John Fenne, Oliver Scott, Luke Astwood,

Thomas Cooper, Edward Dent, Edward Isaac, Nehemiah Coxe, for the furtherance of the worke of God, and carrying on thereof in the meetings usually maintained by this congregation [*i.e.*, in the villages around], as occasion and opportunity shall by Providence be ministered to them."

"The congregation did also determine to keep the 26th of this instant as a day of fasting and prayer, both here and at Hawnes and at Gamlinghay, solemnly to commend to the grace of God bro. Bunyan, bro. Fenne, and the rest of the brethren; and to intreat His gracious assistance and presence with them in their respective worke, whereunto He hath called them."

While turning over these old Church records, a hallowed feeling comes over one. Through the lines of fading ink the undying spirits of the holy dead seem to be looking forth. In their "much seeking of God," in their days of "fasting and prayer," do they not give us the secret of their power—of that noble constancy at which men wonder still?

The temptation to linger yet longer among these old days is strong upon me, but I must forbear, for I greatly fear I have trespassed far already beyond my fitting space. Some other day, if life be spared, I may tell this story, and give these records at greater length. Suffice it now to say, that for the next seventeen years, instant in season and out of season, Bunyan "stood as if he pleaded with men." His ministrations all the country round made him a Bishop indeed. Almost his first act after his liberation was to apply for licences for preachers and preaching places far and near. In the State Paper Office, in a bundle of more than three thousand applications, made from all parts of the country in 1672, I lighted the other day upon the actual sheet which Bunyan sent in, in his own handwriting. He asks for the following licences under the Declaration of Indulgence:—

Bedf.	John Donne,	for his own and the house of George Fowler in Kaishow.
	William Jarvis,	for his owne house in Ridgemont and for George Palmer's house in Cranfield.
	Thos. Kent,	for William Amis, his house in Cranfield.
	John Wright,	for the Lake-house barn in Blunham.
	Nathaniel Alcock,	for John Tingey's house at Ford End.
	John Bunyon,	for Josias Roughead's house in his orchard in Bedford.
	Edward Isaac,	for the house of Gilbert Ashley in Godlington.
	Thomas Cooper,	for the house of William Findon in Okeley.
All Congregationall.	John Sewster,	for the house of John Baxter in Kempston.
	John Whiteman,	for the house of Frances Whiteman, widow, in Cardington.
	John Fenne,	for the house of William Man in Stadgeden.
	Samuel Fenne,	for the house of William Maxey in Hanes.
	Nehemiah Coxe,	for the house of Sarah Tomkins, widow, in Maulden.
	Edward Dent,	for George Pridden's house in Edworth.
	Stephen Hawthorn,	for his own house in Turvy.
	John Allen,	for the house of the Widow Reade in Steventon.
	Daniel Negoos,	for Robert Chine's house in Pavenham.
These by Huntingtonshire.	George Fowler,	for the house of John Cooke in Upthorpe.
	James Rogers,	for the house of John Haynes in Wonditch in Kimbolton Parish.
North Hamptonshire. All Congregationall.	Thos. Brett,	for John Moore, his barn in Wollaston.
	Thos. Edmunds,	for John Brooks' house in Wollaston.
	Christopher Stanley,	for his own house in Brafield-in-the-Green.
Cambridgeshire.	Luke Astwood,	for his own house in Gamlinghay.
	John Waite,	for his own house in Toft.
Herfordshire		for the house of Thos. Morrise in Ashwell.
Bucks.	John Gibbs,	for William Smyth's barn and his own house in Newport Pagnell.
	William Hensman,	for Joseph Kent, his barn in Olney.

Thus with a large-hearted care Bunyan sought to make spiritual provision for all the country round, and while making Bedford the centre of his work, and its Church his special care, during the next seventeen years he was in the habit of preaching far and near; but not without anxieties and threatenings. In the tenth year of his ministry we catch a little glimpse of the state of things at Bedford from the Entering Book of Roger Morrice, who now lies sleeping side by side with Bunyan in Bunhill Fields. This Roger Morrice, after his ejection from Duffield, in Derbyshire, was chaplain to Denzil, Lord Hollis. His manuscripts are compiled chiefly from collections in the library of Lord Hollis, and contain a great many curious things which have never yet seen the light. Among them is the following account of what took place at the Privy Council while Bunyan was minister at Bedford :—

"Mr. Audley, of the Temple, was accused at the counsell table as a very great enemy to the Government, and to the Church of England, and a great countenancer of conventiclers and phanaticks in the town of Bedford where he was Recorder. And though there was many other aldermen disaffected, yet he was the great head and pillar of the disaffected party, and therefore it was moved by the Earl of Aylesbury, Lord-Lieutenant of that county, that he and other aldermen might be displaced by virtue of the Corporation Act. The town was very much troubled at this charge, and old Mr. Audley was prevailed with to appear at the counsell table on behalfe of the town, and did so. He then told His Majestie he was Recorder (I think before the warr), that he was an officer under his father King Charles I. throughout the whole war, that when the war was at an end he was driven out of the kingdome together with his gratious master, that his estate was sequestered, that upon his master the King's restoration he was restored to his estate and to his Recordership and made Justice of the Peace, that he was as truly loyall now as he was then, that he was so far from being a conventicler that he was never at a conventicle in his life, but if the conventiclers preached as well as they were reported to him to doe, and the Churchmen as ill as those did that he heard of late, he did not know but he might go to conventicles, but his acquaintance lay with the opposite faction chiefly; that as he did not desire to be made a Justice of the Peace so did he not say this that he might be continued a Justice of the Peace, for such were put into that commission that he should be almost ashamed to sit upon the bench with. And so the complaint fell, and Mr. Audley went home again." Went home again one would think with the mental satisfaction of a man who feels that on a critical occasion he has held his own and a little more.

This was not the only time that danger threatened the Bedford Church. On the death of Charles, in 1685, and the accession of James, the Nonconformists were made to pass through very trying experiences. Feeling the uncertainty of his position, Bunyan in that year by deed of gift made over to his wife all that he had, so that at least she might not be left utterly destitute were he once more sent to prison as a felon. The document was found in a recess of the house in St. Cuthbert's where he lived, and is duly attested by four witnesses. In it he describes himself as John Bunyan, of the parish of St. Cuthbert's, in the town of Bedford, *brazier*. He has long been a man of power, and could gather his thousands of hearers in London, even in the chill of a winter's morning. Yet there is about him the same grand old simplicity as in the past, and he is John Bunyan, brazier, still.

In less than three years after he signed that deed, he went home to be with God. One night in August, 1688, he made his way to John Strudwick's house on Snow Hill wet with the dripping rain. He was not an old man as the years go, but the stress of life had told on him, and that long wet ride from Reading was more than nature's force could rally from. He was stricken for death, but it was probably some days before the worst symptoms showed themselves, and during that interval he sent the short treatise, "The Acceptable Sacrifice; or, the Excellency of a Broken Heart," to be printed at the Hand and Bible on London Bridge. Some of the proof-sheets he was able to revise, but before the entire book was printed the fever had done its work. The rest of the sheets fell into the hands of an old friend, who, with loving care, did what was needful for this the last child of his brain. John Strudwick, the grocer, was a deacon of the Rev. George Cokayn's Church in Red Cross Street, and George Cokayn was not only an old and valued friend of Bunyan's, but also a Bedfordshire man, a native of Cople, close by Bedford. He was older than Bunyan, and by the Act of Uniformity had been ejected from the famous City Church of Pancras in Soper Lane. During the evil days which followed, he was often among his relatives in Bedfordshire. One Matthew Morgan, of Cardington, thought it worth while to report to the Government what Geo. Cokayn, of Soper Lane, London, had said while preaching and praying at John Cokayn's house in Cardington in the month of January, 1662-3.* He prayed, it seems, "for the deliverance of the godly imprisoned in the nation." The faces of dear friends were present, both to him and the others in that little meeting as thus he prayed. It may be that on his way to Cardington he had called at Bedford gaol, where Bunyan then was, and the thought of his friend had drawn out his heart in prayer. Be that as it may, when Bunyan lay in John Strudwick's house, Cokayn and he had known each other for many a long year, and now at the end Cokayn was there to close the Dreamer's eyes in death. He also saw his friend's last book through the press, and wrote a loving preface to it, telling us how the

---

* State Papers. Domestic. Chas. II. Vol. xci., 22.

Lord had removed that friend, "to the great loss and inexpressible grief of many precious souls." He tells us also that Bunyan had written that book on the "excellency of a broken heart," out of his own heart; for "God, who had much work for him to do, was still hewing and hammering him by His Word, and sometimes also by more than ordinary temptations and desertions." He says this was so, because some thorn in the flesh was needed, and "God in mercy sent it him lest, under his extraordinary circumstances, he should be exalted above measure, which perhaps was the evil that did more easily beset him than any other." With heart-words like these, Cokayn sent forth Bunyan's last book into the world, within a month of the day on which he had buried him in Bunhill Fields. And since Bunyan's dust was not to rest among us in Bedford, but more fittingly, perhaps, in the great city which is the centre of his nation's life, it is a pleasure to Bedfordshire men to feel that it was his old Cople friend who closed his eyes in death, and who read the words of Christian hope over the sleeper in John Strudwick's grave.

JOHN BROWN.

Bedford, July 9th, 1874.

THE FESTIVAL AT BEDFORD,

JUNE 10, 1874.

In 1672, when the "Indulgence" was granted to Dissenters, George Whitehead, the Quaker, prevailed upon King Charles II. to pardon such as were in prison; and the order of release sent to Bedford gaol in the September of that year contained, in addition to eight others, the name of "John Bunnion," who thereupon became the first Nonconformist minister that was licensed to preach in England. Exactly two hundred years after this notable liberation, when the Pilgrim walked forth from the "den" in which he had written the first part of his immortal book, the ninth Duke of Bedford paid a visit to the town whose name he bears for the purpose of opening the Corn Exchange. In a speech to the citizens, his Grace said: "The Mayor of Bedford (Dr. Coombs) wishes me simply to allude to a short conversation I have had with him. I am at this moment having a cast taken for a statue of John Bunyan, who is so closely connected with this town; and if you think it worthy of your acceptance, it will be a great satisfaction to me if you accept it." These simple words of his Grace, uttered in 1872, the bicentenary of Bunyan's release, were heard by all with pleasure, while they sent a thrill through many hearts; for there were present those who knew that the speaker, besides exemplifying in this act the liberal spirit which has always characterised the house of Russell, was prompted to the expression of pious regard for a great memory by the recollection that the first book given to him, when he was a child, by his mother* was the "Pilgrim's Progress." Thus there was in the act that touch of nature which makes the whole world kin: it brought together the child of the peasant and the child of the peer. The proffered statue was seen to be much more than a ducal benefaction, inasmuch as it was an offering from the heart of filial piety. Bedford might well be proud to accept such a gift.

The measure of her pride and joy was seen on Wednesday, the 10th of June, 1874, which had been fixed for the unveiling of the statue. Great were the preparations made by the civic authorities and the people of the good old town. Every political and ecclesiastical distinction was submerged under the flowing tide of a generous emotion that was at once national and Christian in its character. The feeling was warmly shared by all the dwellers in the great tract of fertile country that is watered by the Ouse—a region of England whose quiet natural aspects are strangely blended with moral associations that stir the soul like a trumpet, for it is the land of Cromwell and Bunyan, of Cowper and Howard, of William Carey and Robert Hall; and the crowds that poured into Bedford town on the morning of the eventful day from all the neighbouring shires sufficed to show that the old Puritan spirit is still the ruling power in that province which has been a prolific mother of great men. Nor was the gathering

---

* Francis Charles Hastings Russell, ninth Duke of Bedford, is the son of the late Major-General Lord George William Russell, brother of the seventh Duke, by Elizabeth Anne, only child of the late Hon. John Theophilus Rawdon. The Duke was born October 16, 1819, and succeeded his cousin William, the eighth Duke of Bedford, in 1872. He sat as M.P. for Bedfordshire from 1847 to 1872. His Grace has two brothers—Lord Arthur Russell, M.P. for Tavistock, and Lord Odo Russell, the well-known diplomatist. His Grace married, in 1844, Lady Elizabeth Sackville-West, eldest daughter of the fifth Earl Delawarr, by whom he has issue, living, two sons and two daughters. The mother of the Duke was one of the intimate friends of the late Mrs. Thomas Carlyle, the wife of the distinguished author. In a letter from Mrs. Carlyle to the late Sir George Sinclair, of Ulbster, which has been published in the life of the Baronet, a very interesting reference is made to "Bessie Rawdon."

merely that of a single province; for distant cities in the south and the north sent representatives to take part in the pious festival, and even from the other side of the sea came descendants of the Pilgrim Fathers, rejoicing that they too were members of this good old stock, and could claim to have a family interest in the proceedings of the day.

Preparatory Sermons.

On the preceding Sabbath special sermons had been preached, not only in Nonconformist, but also in some of the Established Churches of the town. At Holy Trinity Church, the Rev. C. A. Greaves, B.C.L., who preached from Matthew xxiii. 27—32, said they were about to unveil the statue of a righteous man, if not to garnish his sepulchre; and there were those who, like the Scribes and Pharisees, should not rejoice that they lived not in the days of their fathers to be partakers with them in persecuting good men. There remained in the present day many who persecuted still. Those who claimed with arrogance all the truth for themselves, whether in a church or a Little Bethel of their own, possessed a harsh spirit, and were the children of those who locked up Bunyan. The preacher urged his hearers to be tolerant as well as faithful in obeying the voice of truth. At Bunyan Meeting, the Rev. J. Brown, B.A., preached from John iv. 37, to a crowded congregation :—

In a few days, he said, they would do special honour to Bunyan's memory, but others would be honoured in him. In 1669 there were in Bedfordshire, with its then scanty population, more than forty conventicles, and more than 1,000 persons in regular attendance upon them. That is to say, after nine long weary years of experience of the Act of Uniformity, of the Conventicle Act, and of the Five-mile Act, there were chiefly in the villages of Bedfordshire more than 1,000 persons, Baptist, Independent, Quaker, and Presbyterian, who still claimed and who still exercised the right to worship God according to their reading of His Word. All honour to them, said he! Some of them were ruined by fines. The farmer saw his wheat carried off and his horses and cattle put up to auction to pay his fines; the tradesman's goods were cleared out of his shop; the workman's tools and housewife's spinning wheel were seized and sold; the skillet in which a poor widow was bearing milk to her two sick children was, the milk being thrown away, borne off in triumph to help to pay the fifteen shillings fine for going to pray with her brethren and sisters who loved the Lord Jesus Christ. All these things and more were done; yet these people held on their way and quietly said, "Whether it be right in the sight of God to hearken unto you more than unto God, judge ye!" We owe much to these godly people of the Puritan days. England would not have been the England she is to-day for us and our children if they had weakly yielded and surrendered their liberties. We owe it to them to maintain the great principles which were dear to their hearts, and we owe it to ourselves, for the blessings of freedom and spiritual life can only be retained while they are kept in the same high spirit in which they were won at first. The greatest honour they could pay to the past was to hold the truth faithfully in the present and hand it on to the future. If the brave old Nonconformist preacher could stand among them on Wednesday next, if he could look at the crowd with those piercing eyes of his that used to look men through and through, he (the preacher) thought he would say, "Friends, this is kind of you, your love gladdens my heart; but above all things be true to that Christ whom I love and who loved me. Read my 'Pilgrim,' with admiration if you will, but above all things be pilgrims yourselves."

Relics of Bunyan.

It was in the spirit of these words that many thousands assembled in Bedford on the morning of the joyful celebration. The people of the town and neighbouring villages, including Elstow, Bunyan's birthplace, made it a holiday; all the shops in the borough were closed; the hospitable burgesses kept open house for friends from a distance; as the morning wore on, the bells of St. Peter's and St. Paul's rang merrily, and thousands of visitors arrived by rail and road. Two arches of evergreens were erected at St. Peter's Green, and flags were displayed on every hand, with mottoes and Scripture texts. The weather in the morning had threatened rain, but before noon all fears on this head were dispelled, and sweet sunshine flashed upon the flags and banners with which the streets were canopied. Many of the visitors took an early drive to Elstow, to see the cottage where the tinker dwelt, or rather the cottage which stands on the same site; and Bunyan Meeting was visited by not a few, who were shown, in a corner of the vestry, the veritable arm-chair in which the famous old pastor of the church used to sit. In the Corn Exchange, where the great meeting of the day was to be held, there had been arranged for inspection some deeply interesting relics—Bunyan's will, found in his house at Bedford, dated December 23, 1685, yellow with age, but the signature distinct; a page from the church records, written by Bunyan himself, stating in clear language and penmanship how certain brethren and sisters were called before the church and admonished for various faults; an edition (dated 1641) of Foxe's "Book of Martyrs," which Bunyan had with him, helping to sustain his soul, in prison, and where on three separate pages he had, in homely verse, recorded his admiration of witnesses who went to the flames; and an antique pint mug used by Bunyan in gaol. There was also the walking-stick which accompanied him on his peregrinations. It is a Malacca cane, and has a large ivory handle curiously inlaid with circlets of silver, the alternate clusters being settings of malachite, while the extremity is preserved by means of an iron ferrule, vandyked at the point of junction with the cane. Besides this, there was Bunyan's cabinet, a quaint, worm-eaten relic that has suffered from the tooth of time, the front of the drawers ornamented with views of a conventional character, the inner side of the door with pictures of musical instruments. This cabinet, and also the jug, was originally in the possession of Mrs. Bithrey, of Carlton, Bunyan's great-granddaughter, and was bequeathed by her, in 1802, to the Rev. Charles Vorley, Baptist minister of Carlton, through whose widow it came into the possession of the trustees of the Bunyan Meeting. Mr. W. W. Kilpin, of Bickerings Park, sent a small round oak table, made from the wood of Bunyan's pulpit. The old edition of Foxe belongs to the Bedford Literary and Scientific Institute; the other articles are in the possession of the trustees of Bunyan Meeting.

The Procession to the Statue.

At a quarter to one o'clock the members of the Corporation and the chief guests assembled at the Council Chamber, where a procession was formed. The route lay through the main thoroughfare of the town, the distance to St. Peter's Green, the site of the statue, being less than half-a-mile. A posse of police led the way, and after them came the Mayor's sergeant and mace-bearers, the bearer of the Mayor's banner, then the Mayor, Mr. Alderman George Hurst, in robes and chain, accompanied by the Lord Lieutenant of Bedfordshire, Earl Cowper, K.G.; and Dr. Stanley, the Dean of Westminster: Dr. Brock, late Baptist minister at Bloomsbury Chapel, London; Mr. C. M. Birrell, late Baptist minister at Pembroke Chapel, Liverpool; and Dr. Henry Allon, Independent minister at Union Chapel, Islington : Mr. F. Bassett, M.P. for Bedfordshire; Mr. Samuel Whitbread and Captain F. C. Polhill-Turner, the members for the borough: the Deputy-Mayor, Mr. Councillor Young, with Mr. H. Young, jun., Pimlico, the founder who cast the statue : past Mayors, Messrs. W. W. Kilpin, Thos. Barnard, W. J. Nash, James Howard, R. Couchman, A. E. Burch, Dr. Coombs, Alderman Gray, and J. R. Bull: Aldermen Jessopp, Sergeant, and Carter : town councillors, Messrs. W. Harrison, J. Colburne (Capt.), J. Barrand, W. Roff, J. E. Cutcliffe, J. Horsford, T. Bull, H. Thody, A. G. Shelton, and W. Roberts: county magistrates, Col. W. B. Higgins, Pictshill; Mr. J. N. Foster, Sandy Place; Mr. G. Higgins, Castle Close, Bedford; Mr. W. F. Higgins, Turvey House, and Mr. Magniac, Colworth House: borough magistrates, Messrs. W. H. Jackson, T. S. Trapp, Frederick Howard, T. J. Jackson, and J. T. Wing: Dr. Prior, the borough coroner, and Mr. J. Wyatt, F.G.S., the borough treasurer : Mr. R. E. Roberts, the gaoler; and other officers of the Corporation. These were followed by residents and visitors, including the Rev. F. Fanshawe, head-master of the Bedford Grammar School ; Rev. C. Brereton, rector of St. Mary's, and rural dean ; Rev. J. Brown, B.A., minister of Bunyan Meeting; Rev. J. Copner, vicar of Elstow ; Rev. J. Frost, of the Cotton End Training Institute ; Rev. J. Stoughton, D.D., London; Rev. W. H. Smith, rector of St. Peter's ; Messrs. Edwin Ransom and T. G. E. Elger, members of the Inauguration Committee ; Revs. R. Speed, Baptist; J. J. Rew, chaplain of the county prison; C. E. Satcliffe, Moravian ; Canon Warmoll, Roman Catholic; W. Parker Irving, Howard Chapel; H.

Jones and F. Hewitt, Wesleyans; and D. Cartwright, Catholic Apostolic Church; Mr. J. S. Wright, Birmingham; Rev. E. Jeffery; Rev. T. Arnold, Congregationalist, Northampton; Messrs. R. B. Stafford, M. Sharman, R. Hill, J. F. Nutter, and E. Coleman; Capt. Toseland; Rev. H. Wood, vicar of Biddenham; Major Benning, Dunstable; Mr. F. Wykes, Ravensden; Mr. Gutteridge, Dunstable; Mr. C. W. Ryalls, LL.D., London; Hon. Mr. Coke, &c.

The Unveiling of the Statue.

St. Peter's Green, the site chosen by the sculptor himself for the statue, was reached at half-past one; but so great was the pressure of the crowd in the streets that the procession was cut in two, and the last half came struggling through the throng into the enclosure in somewhat sorry plight. A gaily decorated platform, which afforded standing room for 200 persons, had been erected in the rear of the statue. On one side were a large number of ladies; and on the other the officials and their guests, the latter including many ministers, both of the Established and Free Churches, who did not walk in the procession, also the venerable Mr. John Howard, of Bedford, and Mr. J. E. Boehm, the sculptor. The metropolitan and provincial press sent twenty-five representatives, these including Mr. James Clarke, the Editor of the *Christian World*; and reporters were present from the London offices of the *New York Tribune* and the *Herald* of the same city. The ceremony of unveiling the statue did not occupy many minutes. First of all the Mayor made a speech, showing how the chief glory of Bedford is the name of Bunyan, and praising their good Duke for his munificence. One of his remarks merits special note—that a statue has comparatively a limited moral power, unless it be placed in a locality that is intimately connected with the person whom it commemorates. At his Worship's invitation, the Lady Augusta Stanley, wife of the Dean of Westminster, and a sister of the late Earl of Elgin, gracefully advances and unveils the statue. Ringing cheers from ten thousand voices greet the appearance of what is perceived at a glance to be one of the noblest works of the kind in England; the band plays the National Anthem, and silence only is restored when the Mayor requests the company to be perfectly still for a minute or two, until the scene shall have been caught by the photographer's art. Then follows a speech from Dean Stanley, perhaps the shortest and most effective that was ever delivered on such an occasion. It consisted of the following sentences:—

The Mayor has called upon me to say a few words, and I shall obey him. The Mayor has done his work, the Duke of Bedford has done his, the sculptor and artist have done theirs, and now I ask you to do yours in commemorating John Bunyan. Every one of you who has not read the "Pilgrim's Progress," if there be any such person, read it without delay; those who have read it a hundred times, read it for the hundred and first time. Follow out in your lives the lessons which the "Pilgrim's Progress" teaches, and then you will all of you be even better monuments of John Bunyan than this magnificent statue which the Duke of Bedford has given you.

Mr. John Bright was expected to come, but he has written to say that on account of the state of his health he dare not venture; and so his Birmingham chairman, Mr. J. S. Wright, takes his place, and not only as a man of the people, but also as a representative of the Baptists of Birmingham, expresses his joy. He confessed the scene was to him like a story in the "Arabian Nights," and he had been especially gladdened to hear the ringing of the church bells. This speech closed the ceremony of unveiling at five minutes to two; and as the vast gathering slowly separated, cheers were given with the utmost enthusiasm for Lady Augusta Stanley, the Duke and Duchess of Bedford, and one cheer for the Mayor.

The Statue.

We are now at liberty to survey the work of art which has brought us to Bedford. It is a production of Herr J. E. Boehm. The figure is ten feet high, and contains about two and a-half tons of bronze. It was cast of cannon and bells lately brought from China. The likeness of Bunyan is taken from a contemporary painting by Sadler, now in the possession of the Rev. Mr. Clive. The costume is that of the Puritans of Bunyan's day—the long cloak, with tight-buttoned tunic, broad collar, and knee breeches. The idea which the sculptor has striven to work out is embodied in the inscription at the back of the pedestal, which is taken from Bunyan's description of the picture he saw hung up against the wall in Interpreter's house of "a very grave person." The lines on the pedestal run thus :—

> "It had eyes uplifted to heaven;
> The best of books in his hand;
> The law of truth was written
> Upon his lips. . . .
> It stood as if it pleaded
> With men."*

---

* It has been questioned whether this is the most judicious choice that could have been made to describe the *motif* of the artist; and the quotation is certainly inaccurate, inasmuch as it gives the word "it," instead of "he," in the first and fifth lines. The extract was suggested as a faithful description of the statue by the Rev. James Copner, M.A., vicar of Elstow, in the preface, dated February 19, 1874, to "The Hero of Elstow; or, the Story of the Pilgrimage of John Bunyan." Mr. Copner was not aware whether the sculptor, when preparing his design, had in his memory these words of Interpreter.

The "glorious dreamer" is standing in a most natural attitude, holding an open Bible in his left hand, the fingers of his right hand resting upon the page. His face, turned upwards, yet not averted from the persons with whom he is supposed to be pleading, is radiant with the truth he is setting forth. There is, perhaps, less of robust vigour in the expression than we look for in a man of Bunyan's mould, and a more strongly pronounced smile than would often be seen lighting up features which are described by contemporaries as habitually grave, and even stern; yet the moment seized by the artist is one in which implicit faith and exultant joy are animating the soul of the preacher as he tenderly pleads with men, and there cannot be two opinions as to the strong moral impression which the countenance of this earnest preacher is calculated to make on the beholder. The effect is exceedingly vivid and pleasing. A broken fetter at his feet typifies the imprisonment to which for twelve years he was doomed for the heinous offence of preaching. His right foot is forward, the left being in close proximity to the stone pillar on which the prison shackles lie. The lengthy locks droop in curls over his shoulders, and the moustaches are twirled sharply upwards. On the bronze tablet beneath the figure is a bold copy of the autograph, "John Bunyan," a *fac-simile* of the one appended to his will. On the front and two sides of the pedestal are scenes in very bold relief from the "Pilgrim's Progress." The front one represents the termination of Christian's fight with Apollyon; the left illustration shows Evangelist directing Christian to the wicket-gate*; the right the Pilgrim's release from his load, and the three Shining Ones pointing out to him the

---

* Some think the wicket-gate should not have been represented by a common country field-gate; indeed, that it should not have been introduced in any shape into the picture, since Christian could not see it. It has also been pointed out as a defect—but it is certainly a trivial one —that the Pilgrim in two of the relievos is represented as wearing a moustache, while in the third he has none.

Celestial City. The **relievos**, like the statue, deserve the most **cordial praise, and will** doubtless inspire salutary **thoughts** in many a **heart.** The statue is placed at the south-west corner of **St. Peter's Green, where** four **roads meet.** The picturesque church of **St.** Peter with the **trees** form a pretty background. The **statue is surrounded** by a railing, consisting of massive stone pillars and an elegant chain ; **and** the railings of the green **have been** diverted and carried behind the statue. The **opinion has** been expressed that **the** pedestal, especially **its plinth, is too** small in proportion to the colossal **size of the figure that** surmounts it. Take it for **all in all, however, we do** not know that **we can** point **to a work of the kind in** this country which we regard **as more successful.**

Meeting in the Exchange.

Of course the brief talk **on the green could not suffice as an** expression of the **emotion** with which every **heart was** charged ; **and** this found **vent** in a great meeting **held at** three o'clock in the Corn **Exchange, and which** lasted for **upwards of two hours. Admission was by ticket, and the** building **was crammed to the utmost limit of its capacity.** Rarely, if ever, have we heard better addresses, or seen a more sympathetic **audience ; and the delightful unity** of feeling exhibited **from first to last was a** foretaste of **that** happy **time for which so many are** praying and working—"**and come it will, for a' that**"—when the principles **which John** Bunyan **expounded will take** possession **of the nation's** heart and rule **the life of** England. Before **formally opening the** meeting, **the Mayor** mentioned that **he had received letters** from various distinguished **persons who had intended, but were** unable, **to be** present. Lord

3

Shaftesbury was to have taken part in the unveiling of the statue, but Archbishop Tait's Bill for the repression of Ritualism had detained him at Westminster. Baroness Burdett-Coutts, Lord Mayor Lusk, the Lord Provost of Glasgow, the Mayor of Southampton (Mr. Edwin Jones) and the Mayor of Salisbury, Colonel Gilpin, M.P., the Revs. C. H. Spurgeon, of London; H. Stowell Brown, of Liverpool; Alexander M'Laren, B.A., of Manchester; R. W. Dale, C. Vince, and George Dawson, of Birmingham; R. R. Suffield, of Croydon; Mr. Edward Maitland, author of "The Pilgrim and the Shrine," and Sir Charles Reed, were among the apologists. The last-named sent a letter of such interest that it was read to the meeting. Sir Charles desired that attention should be called to the name of Thomas Marsom, the Luton ironmonger, who succoured Bunyan, and declined release that he might remain Bunyan's fellow-prisoner in Bedford gaol, and from whose daughter Mr. Russell Gurney, the Recorder of London, claims to be directly descended. The Mayor then made a somewhat elaborate speech, in which he expressed his belief—herein, by the way, agreeing with Macaulay—that Bunyan, in the depth of his remorse, exaggerated his own vices. He also lauded him for the absence from his works of all political bias. Dean Stanley's address, which was probably the very happiest of his efforts as a platform speaker, occupied nearly three-quarters of an hour in the delivery, and was listened to with rapt attention and frequent bursts of applause. Both as to its substance and style, it was simply perfection, and even the ecclesiastical aspects of Bunyan's life were so felicitously reviewed that not a single Nonconformist present could have felt any inclination to be critical. With a sly touch of sarcasm, that excited loud laughter, especially from the strangers, the Dean set out by saying that the only title of Bedford to universal and lasting fame was derived from the fact that it contained the "den" in which the immortal Pilgrim was imprisoned—an equivocal compliment which, for the moment, gave a sober expression to the faces of the local dignitaries, but this wore away almost immediately as the speaker proceeded to sketch, with fine pictorial effect, the local aspects of the great dreamer's life. The generous tribute paid to the Church of which Bunyan was a minister elicited much applause, and cheers, mingled with hearty laughter, greeted the reference to the decrepid condition of old Intolerance. The Dean expressed his satisfaction that this old giant, who was very stout and hearty in Bunyan's time, was now disabled, he hoped, for ever. Hereupon the audience, and especially one exuberant spirit on the platform, burst into an eager cheer. "Ah," interposed the Dean, with a good-natured smile, "don't be too jubilant, my friends. The old giant is still alive"—this with a humorous touch that provoked shouts of laughter; "he may be seen on all sides; the spirits of burning and judgment have not altogether departed from mankind, either from Churchmen or Nonconformists; but the giant's joints are very stiff and crazy." Next came a splendid eulogium of Bunyan's most famous book. This was followed by a graphic sketch of the man Bunyan, and the peroration of the address was a touching appeal, in which we were asked to remember that the pilgrimage described by Bunyan is the experience of every one of us.

The next speaker was Earl Cowper, the Lord-Lieutenant of the county, whose brief address preserved the happy tone struck in the key-note of the Dean. Indeed, the noble layman's strain was in one sense an improvement upon that of the ecclesiastic; for he did not hesitate to avow that, as a Churchman, he felt humiliation and shame when he reflected on the part played by his Church towards John Bunyan.

The feeling that the millennium had arrived, and that instead of being in a Corn Exchange in an English county town we were in a much better place, became almost too strong to be resisted when we saw the Earl followed by a Baptist preacher of the Bunyan type—the Mayor, who is a Churchman, introducing Dr. Brock as his friend. Nor had his Worship any cause given him to be ashamed of this frank confession. The ex-pastor of Bloomsbury carries a letter of introduction in his face which no audience in England would refuse to honour. He stepped forward, a truly typical Briton; and in his speech there was the blunt sincerity and fearlessness which John Bull always respects. On such an occasion there is a temptation to speak only a part of the truth, and on the other hand a danger of saying too much. Dr. Brock, trusting doubtless to the spontaneous feeling of the moment, said neither too little nor too much. He hit the golden mean, and was as loudly applauded by Churchmen as by Dissenters. Very fine was his tribute to the house of Russell, his panegyric on the Lady Rachel, which came from the heart, bringing tears to many eyes; but the main part of his speech was a vigorous plea for religious equality.

The Baptist was followed by a representative of the other branch of the great Congregational family; and Dr. Allon's paper deserved to be bracketed with that of Dean Stanley as the literary treat of the day. It was chiefly devoted to a review of the characteristics of Bunyan as an author, and claimed for him a greater spontaneity than was exhibited even by Shakespeare, and the distinction of being the author of the first English novel. His merits as a theologian and as a sacred orator were also glanced at by the essayist.

In a speech, uniting modesty with manly dignity, the Rev. J. Brown, B.A., minister of Bunyan Meeting, moved a vote of thanks to the Duke of Bedford for his gift. The way in which this was done was worthy of one who stands in the pulpit occupied two centuries ago by John Bunyan. It is saying much to assert that Mr. Brown sustained, in the estimation of the great assembly, the perilous honour with which he is invested; and yet it is the simple truth.* Profound interest was excited by his statement that Bunyan's church was founded on the principle, still observed, of requiring from members simply faith in Christ and holiness of life, without respect to this or that circumstance or opinion in outward and circumstantial things. "On this truly catholic basis," exclaimed Mr. Brown, "and not on that of mere ecclesiastical organisation, may the Church of the future stand!"—a sentiment which was loudly cheered. The Rev. James Copner, Vicar of Elstow, who has lately published a sketch of Bunyan's life, seconded the resolution of thanks, which was carried with great heartiness; and the Hundredth Psalm having been sung, Dean Stanley pronounced the benediction, with which the meeting was brought to a close.

Open-Air Meetings.

There were of course thousands of people in the town who could not find admission to the Corn Exchange; but they were provided for by a happy thought of some Baptist friends, who arranged for two great open-air meetings. As soon as the Mayor knew of their intention, he kindly placed the platform and gallery erected for the

---

* Mr. Brown will forgive the Editor of the present volume for here relating an anecdote which would have delighted the late genial and truly venerable Dean Ramsay, of Edinburgh, who for so many years was the Stanley of the Scotch Episcopal Church. An esteemed minister of Bunyan Chapel, during a Scottish tour, visited Glenlyon, where he was introduced by a friend to a worthy Highlander as "Bunyan's successor." The Highlandman looked at the stranger from top to toe, and exclaimed, "Eh, mon! but you'll have hard work to fill *his* shoon!"

unveiling at their disposal. Most of the speakers had not been fully apprised of the design till after they arrived at Bedford; yet the speeches were varied and effective, giving historic references, striking citations from the life and works of Bunyan, practical lessons, and salutary counsels. Appreciative attention was paid to the speakers, both by the hundreds of people that stood around, and by many persons at the windows of adjacent houses. The afternoon meeting, presided over by Mr. J. Pratt, of Bedford, lasted from three till four; and the speakers were the Revs. T. Voysey, of Sandy, and W. Abbott, of Blunham; Mr. G. Gunton, of Bedford; Mr. John Longland, of Yardley Hastings; and Mr. William Ashton, of Uxbridge. The evening meeting, at six o'clock, was also presided over by Mr. Pratt, and very numerously attended. The first speaker was the Rev. A. C. Gray, of Luton. "Most of you," he said, "are Bedfordshire people, and may well be proud of John Bunyan. I was born nearly 500 miles from Bedford, but, in my boyhood, used to read the 'Pilgrim's Progress,' and think of John Bunyan and Elstow, where he was born, in the same way, only in a lesser degree, as I thought of the Holy Land, where the prophets wrote and spake. One of the first visits I made after coming to Bedfordshire was to Elstow, to see the cottage, or a relic of the cottage, where Bunyan lived. And I marvelled not to find, from the record of visitors kept there, that great numbers from the east and west, from the north and south of the United Kingdom and from America, came to see that cottage; for crowds, through Bunyan, all over the world, have started on the grandest of all pilgrimages—leaving the City of Destruction to tread the path to Heaven." The Rev. J. W. Genders, of Luton, directed attention to the leading characteristics of Bunyan as a man and a preacher; and the Rev. W. Hillier, Mus. Doc., of Ridgemount, spoke of Bunyan as a writer, naming his different works up to sixty, one for each year of his life. He also, in a very effective manner, cited the testimonies of learned men with respect to Bunyan's literary genius—that of Dr. Johnson, who read the "Pilgrim's Progress" through, and wished it longer; **of Dean Swift, who** read it with delight; of Lord Macaulay, who pronounced its writer an original genius; of Dr. **John** Owen, who told Charles II. he would give up all his learning for the power to preach and write like the tinker; of Dr. Arnold, who **thought** Bunyan the best writer of English; of Toplady, who pronounced the allegory the finest extant; of Southey, **and** many others, including **Dean Stanley, Dr. Brock, and Dr.** Allon. The other speakers were Mr. **Attack, of** Hockliffe, and Messrs. **J. Usher and G. Gunton,** of Bedford. All the speakers made reference, in grateful expressions, to the generous and noble gift of the **Duke of Bedford.** By these meet**ings the multitude** found suitable vent for their emotions, **while at** the same time they heard **the** Gospel proclaimed with tenderness and power at the foot of the newly-unveiled statue of John Bunyan. Though not in the programme, this was a feature without which the day's proceedings would hardly have been complete.

Treat to the Children.

During the afternoon about 4,000 **children of the** Sunday-schools in Bedford **and Elstow** were entertained at tea, each one of them receiving an illustrated copy of the "Pilgrim's Progress" as a memorial of the day. A staff of **350 teachers, under the** direction of Mr. W. B. Graham, late **deputy** chief-constable of the county, took the super**vision of the little ones.** A ton and a quarter of cake was provided, and six butts of **tea,** each containing 100 gallons.

There was a grand procession, in which precedence was given to the scholars from Elstow, Bunyan's birthplace, the Church and Dissenting children walking side by side, under the leadership and care of Mr. W. J. Robinson. After the Elstow schools, the Primitive Methodist school of Bedford came first, and the Catholic Apostolic school brought up the rear. Grace was said before tea by the Rev. C. Brereton, rector of St. Mary's; and not less than 5,000 people were present in the field, pleased spectators of a union which, we hope, will seem less strange to the rising generation when they grow up than it did to their fathers. Three bands discoursed music for the pleasure of the children, and the Mayor and Mr. Whitbread, M.P., came to see the happy gathering. The clergyman and teachers of St. Paul's Church school refused to take part in the festival, on grounds which they call religious; but the children of the school, happily innocent of sectarian scruples, came, and were attended to by the teachers of other schools. The arrangements for this gigantic tea-party were carried out by Messrs. J. B. Sergeant, J. U. Taylor, P. S. Fry, J. Atkins, S. Ward, George Carruthers, J. Curtis, Roff, and J. Harris, with Mr. Hillhouse as secretary.

Lecture by Rev. C. M. Birrell.

At seven o'clock there was a large gathering at Bunyan Meeting to hear a lecture on Bunyan by the Rev. C. M. Birrell, late of Liverpool. Mr. Birrell gave the substance of the lecture in the same place in 1853. To not a few this charming address was, perhaps, the chief source of pleasure in the whole of the proceedings. It was grateful, after the bustle of the day, to retire from the crowd into the quietness of the Meeting, with all its hallowed memories of the immortal dreamer; and in this still hour of meditation, who better fitted to speak to us than Mr. Birrell? Though the lecture occupied more than two hours, it was with the greatest reluctance that strangers, obliged to catch trains before its close, could tear themselves away when the lecturer paused to give them an opportunity for retiring. One happy feature of Mr. Birrell's lecture was its exhibition of the fact that to the Society of Friends must be ascribed the merit of securing Bunyan's liberation; and it was meet that this obligation to the Quakers should be publicly acknowledged on such a day, which it would not have been but for Mr. Birrell's wise provision. Cordial thanks were given to the lecturer by the congregation, on the motion of the Rev. J. Brown. A suggestion by Mr. Birrell that Bedford should erect a statue to its second great citizen, John Howard, was hailed with loud cheers.

The Hospitalities of the Day.

We have already said that the burgesses kept open house for their friends; and we ought to add that 100 guests were entertained at luncheon by Mr. Edwin Ransom, the proprietor of the *Bedfordshire Times*. In the evening the Mayor entertained about eighty guests at dinner at the Swan Hotel; and after an elegant repast a most interesting toast list was gone through. Dr. Brock, along with a local clergyman, the Rev. W. H. Smith, responded for "The Bishop of the Diocese and the Ministers of Religion." Dr. Brock said he believed if John Bunyan were at that gathering he would be quite at home in responding to the toast, as according to Mr. Offor he was Chaplain to the Lord Mayor of London after he came out of prison. The toast of the evening, "The Memory of John Bunyan," was proposed by the Rev. Dr. Stoughton in an interesting speech, and drank in silence. Mr. Bassett, M.P., gave the Lord Lieutenant's health, to which Earl Cowper replied, closing his speech with a toast to the Duke of Bedford. Colonel Higgins proposed the toast of the Duchess, and incidentally remarked, as a layman, that he would not say Bedford had gone mad about Bunyan—he believed it had only just come to its senses. Dr. Coombs, ex-Mayor of Bedford, proposed the health of Herr Boehm, the sculptor; and Mr. F. T. Young, vice-chairman, responded to the toast of the Mayor and Corporation. Among the other speakers were the representatives of Bedford in Parliament, Mr. Whitbread and Captain Polhill-Turner, Mr. Magniac, ex-Member for St. Ives, and Mr. James Howard, formerly Member for the borough, and who, with his excellent brother, was foremost in making the preparations for a day that must ever be looked back upon as one of the most memorable in the annals of the town. Opposite the hotel, on the other side of the river, there was a display of fireworks after dark; and this was closed with a magnificent centre piece, which brought out, in letters of fire, the name of JOHN BUNYAN.

In addition to those whose names have been already mentioned, many representative men from various parts of the country were present. The Baptists of the Biggleswade district were represented by the Rev. Philip Griffiths. Oliver Cromwell's native town sent the Rev. J. H. Millard, B.A., secretary of the Baptist Union, and Mr. M. Foster, in the house of whose ancestors John Bunyan used to preach at night when he was under the ban of the law.* Cambridge

---

* During the reigns of Charles II. and James II., the house of the Fosters at Preston, near Hitchin, was an asylum for persecuted ministers. There John Bunyan, when not in Bedford gaol, used to make his home in preaching excursions about the neighbourhood, and not a few

was represented by the Rev. J. P. Campbell; Kettering by Mr. Toller and Mr. Myers; and Ramsey, the parish in the Fens from which the Cromwell family sprang, by Mr. Arthur J. Saunders. The Rev. A. M. Stalker, of Southport, was present; and with Mr. J. S. Wright was Mr. Keep, of Birmingham. Mr. J. Carvell Williams, secretary of the Liberation Society; Sir S. G. Payne, Bart., of Blunham House; the Rev. S. Thornton, of St. George's, Birmingham; Mr. Alderman Swayne, of Leicester; and Mr. Edward Barr, of Leamington, were also among the visitors.

The Prisoner of Bedford.

BY ALDERMAN GEORGE HURST,
Mayor of Bedford.

We have to-day a vast assemblage of people who have come from various parts to witness the interesting ceremony of inaugurating the munificent gift of his Grace the Duke of Bedford, attracted by the universal **reputation of** the subject of the memorial, and **if this room had been** sufficiently spacious (though now of **magnificent proportions**) it might have been filled with **five times the number** here assembled. The early life of Bunyan seems to have been a career of alternate irregularity and despondency—despondency arising from an extremely sensitive and con-

---

are the traditions still preserved in the family of the occasions when they had the joy and honour of entertaining this great genius and apostle of the Church as their guest. Mr. Michael Foster, ex-Mayor of Huntingdon, and the father of Professor Michael Foster, of Cambridge, is the senior survivor of the senior branch of the family. The Fosters of Cambridge, the well-known bankers, whose name is familiar to all who **have** read the biographies of Robert Robinson and Robert Hall, **are also** descendants of John Bunyan's host at Preston, at which place **an effort** is being made, which promises to be crowned with speedy success, **to** erect a place of worship, to be called Bunyan Chapel. The scheme, on the suggestion of Mr. Foster, of Huntingdon, **is** being largely assisted by all the branches of the Foster family.

scientious organism, and it is fair to affirm that his delinquencies were far less atrocious than he himself seemed to imagine. This idiosyncrasy led him almost wholly to religious considerations, and he displayed during his life scarcely any political bias, unlike the other great genius of that period, John Milton, who was the powerful defender of the Parliament and Republicanism. During the struggle between the Parliament and the King, John Bunyan was in the Royalist army, and probably, from his Scriptural reading, he became convinced that he had supported the righteous cause, as we do not find in his works the slightest hints, even when he suffered such severe persecution under the Restoration, of regret that he had fought in the cause of Royalty. During his imprisonment he composed his popular work the "Pilgrim's Progress" and other equally original and excellent books, and it is remarkable that the highest works of human genius have all had religion as their object, and have been produced under circumstances of great affliction. If we go back to remote antiquity—nearly three thousand years—to the

"Immortal dream that could beguile
The blind old man of Scio's rocky isle,"

down to more modern times, when Milton dictated his sublime poems to be written down by the hands of his daughters, these two grand poems that have never been equalled, were composed under the afflicting circumstances of blindness. It would seem that corporeal "light denied," the mental vision became more clear, pure, and intensified. The two most renowned poets of Italy suffered much from tyranny and oppression. Dante was banished, and was for many years a wanderer from the country he dearly loved—a country whose greatest renown and pride is of having been his birthplace. The stern old exile underwent great affliction, composed his "Divina Commedia;" and the other name, of unfading reputation, Tasso, from imputed madness, was confined for many years within the gloomy restriction of a madhouse, where he in imagination

"Revelled among men and things Divine,
And poured his spirit over Palestine,
In honour of the sacred war for Him,
The God who was on earth and is in heaven."

And John Bunyan during an imprisonment for twelve

tedious years was enabled, besides labouring for his family, to conceive his unequalled allegory, and which with freedom he could never have accomplished. As a preacher he was a man of stern, powerful, and unusual eloquence. When he preached at his chapel in this town, or in any of the surrounding villages, though they were at that time but thinly populated, he attracted immense crowds, who came many miles to listen to his discourses, and when in London such was his popularity his congregation numbered thousands of individuals. Then if he had been at liberty the claims for his services would have allowed him but little leisure for literary achievements. The two men of transcendent genius of that period were John Milton and John Bunyan, and the great work of one seems naturally to follow the other. Milton described the fall of angelic beings, and man's first disobedience that "brought death into the world and all our woe." Bunyan, finding man in a state of destruction, makes his Christian escape from thence to pursue his hard and difficult pilgrimage to recover the blessedness that had been sacrificed ; he passes onward through troubles and anxieties, sometimes desponding, at others deviating from his course, to again endure trouble, but frequently receiving support and encouragement from the Evangelist—the blessed Gospel,—but in his way sinking down into the misery of despair, again emerging, and with determination continuing his way onwards, till, travelling the gloomy valley of the shadow of death, he ultimately sinks into the dark waves of death and oblivion, to emerge from thence a beatified spirit, and his griefs and wanderings being over, he is received into the mansions of the blessed to enjoy an eternity of unalloyed happiness.

The Character of John Bunyan:
LOCAL, ECCLESIASTICAL, UNIVERSAL.
BY THE REV. A. P. STANLEY, D.D.,
Dean of Westminster.

"As I walked through the wilderness of this world I lighted upon a certain place where was a den." These words have been translated into hundreds of languages, and hundreds and thousands in all parts of the world and all classes of mankind have asked, "Where was that place, and where was that den?" and the answer has been given that the name of the "place" was Bedford, and that the "den" was Bedford gaol. This it is which has given to the town of Bedford its chief—may I say, without offence, its only title to universal and everlasting fame. It is now two hundred years ago since Bunyan must have resolved on the great venture—so it seemed to him—of publishing the work which has given to Bedford this immortal renown; and Bedford is this day endeavouring to pay back some part of the debt which it owes to him.

It has seemed to me that I should best discharge the trust with which I have been honoured—and a very high honour I consider it to be—by saying a few words, first on the local, then on the ecclesiastical and political circumstances, and then on the universal character of your illustrious townsman.

1. I shall not, in speaking of the local claims of Bunyan, surrender without a struggle the share which England at large has in those claims. Something of a national, something even of a cosmopolitan colour, was given to his career by the wandering gipsy life which drew the tinker with his humble wares from his brazier's shop, as well as by the more serious circuits which he made as an itinerant pastor on what were regarded as his episcopal visitations. When I leave Bedford this evening in order to go to Leicester, I shall still be on the track of the young soldier, who, whether in the Royal or the Parliamentary army — for

it is still matter of dispute—so narrowly escaped the shot which laid his comrade low; and from the siege of its ancient walls gathered the imagery for the "Holy War" and the "Siege of Mansoul." When it was my lot years ago to explore the Pilgrims' Way to Canterbury, I was tempted to lend a willing ear to the ingenious officer on the Ordnance Survey, who conjectured that in that devious pathway and on those Surrey downs the Pilgrim of the seventeenth century may have caught the idea of the Hill Difficulty and the Delectable Mountains. On the familiar banks of the Kennett, at Reading, I recognise the scenes to which tradition has assigned his secret visits, disguised in the slouched hat, white smock frock, and carter's whip of a waggoner, as well as the last charitable enterprise which cost him his life. In the great Babylon of London I find myself in the midst of what must have given him his notion of Vanity Fair; where also, as the Mayor has reminded you, he attracted thousands round his pulpit at Zoar Chapel in Southwark, and where he rests at last in the grave of his host, the grocer Strudwick, in the cemetery of Bunhill Fields.

But none of these places can compete for closeness of association with his birthplace at Elstow. The cottage, or what might have been the cottage of his early home—the venerable church where first he joined in the prayers of our public worship—the antique pew where he sat—the massive tower whose bells he so lustily rang till struck by the pangs of a morbid conscience—the village green where he played his rustic games and was haunted by his terrific visions—the puddles in the road on which he thought to try his first miracles—all these are still with us. And even Elstow can hardly rival the den—whether the legendary prison on the bridge or the historical prison not far from where his monument stands—for which the whole world inquiringly turns to Bedford. Most fitting, therefore, has it been that the first statue erected to the memory of the most illustrious citizen of Bedford should have been the offering of the noble head of the illustrious house to which Bedford has given its chief title. Most fitting it is that St. Peter's Green at Bedford should in this way—if I may use an expression I have myself elsewhere employed—have been annexed to the Poet's Corner of Westminster Abbey, **and should** contain the one effigy which England possesses of the first of human allegorists. Claim **him**, citizens of Bedford and inhabitants of Bedfordshire; **claim** him as your own. It is the strength of a county **and of a town** to have its famous men held in everlasting **remembrance.** They are the links by which you are bound to the history of your country, and by which the whole consciousness of a great nation is bound together. In your Bedfordshire lanes he doubtless found the original of his "**Slough of Despond.**" In the halls and gardens of Wrest, of Haynes, and Woburn, he may have snatched the first glimpses of his "**House Beautiful.**" In the turbid waters of your Ouse at flood time he saw the likeness of the "River Very Deep," which had to be crossed before reaching the Celestial City. You have become immortal through him; see that his glory never fades away amongst you.

2. And here this local connection passes into an ecclesiastical association on which I would dwell for a few moments. If Elstow was the natural birthplace of Bunyan, he himself would certainly have named as his spiritual birthplace the meeting-house at Bedford and the stream of the Ouse, near the corner of Duck Mill Lane, where he was in middle life re-baptized. There, and in those dells of Wainwood and Samsell, where in the hard times he secretly ministered to his scattered flock, he became the most famous preacher of the religious communion which claims him as its own. The Baptist or Ana-baptist Church, which once struck **terror by its very name** throughout the States of Europe, now, and even in Bunyan's time, subsiding into a quiet, loyal, peaceful **community**, has numbered on its roll many illustrious names—a Havelock amongst its soldiers, a Carey and a Marshman among its missionaries, a Robert Hall among its preachers, and I speak now only of the dead. But neither amongst the dead nor the living who have adorned the Baptist name is there any before whom other churches bow their heads so reverently as he who in this place derived his chief spiritual inspirations from them; and amongst their titles to a high place in English Christendom, the conversion of John Bunyan is their chief and sufficient guarantee. We ministers and members of the National Church have much

whereof to glory. We boast, and we justly boast, that one
of our claims on the grateful affection of our country
is that our institutions, our learning, our liturgy, our
version of the Bible, have sustained and enlarged the
general culture even of those who dissent from much
that we teach and from much that we hold dear. But
we know that even this boast is not ours exclusively.
You remember Lord Macaulay's saying that the seventeenth century produced in England two men only of
original genius. These were both Nonconformists—one
was John Milton, and the other was John Bunyan. I will
venture to add this yet further remark, that the whole of
English literature has produced only two prose works of
universal popularity, and both of these also were by Nonconformists—one is the work of a Presbyterian journalist,
and it is called "Robinson Crusoe;" and the other is the
work of a Baptist preacher, and its name is the "Pilgrim's Progress." Every time that we open those well-
known pages, or look at that memorable face, they remind
us Churchmen that Nonconformists have their own splendid
literature; they remind you Nonconformists that literature
and culture are channels of grace no less spiritual than
sacraments or doctrines, than preaching or revivals. There
were many bishops eminent for their piety and learning in
the seventeenth century; but few were more deserving of
the name than he who by the popular voice of Bedfordshire
was called Bishop Bunyan.

3. And now, having rendered honour to whom honour
is due—honour to the town of Bedford, and honour to
my Nonconformist brethren—let me take that somewhat
wider survey to which, as I have said, this occasion
invites me; only let me, before entering on that survey,
touch for an instant on the contrast which is presented by
the recollections of which we have just been speaking, and
the occasion which brings us here together. There are
certain places which we pass by in the valley of life,
like to that which the Pilgrim saw, in which two giants
dwelt of old time, "who," he says, "were either dead many
a day, or else, by reason of age, have grown so crazy and
stiff in their joints that they now do little more than sit at
their cave's mouth, grinning at pilgrims as they go by."
It is at such a cave's mouth that we are to-day. We see at

the long distance of two hundred years, a giant who, in Bunyan's time, was very stout and hearty. What shall we call him? His name was Old Intolerance, that giant who first, under the Commonwealth, in the shape of the Presbyterian clergy, could not bear with "the preaching of an illiterate tinker and an unordained minister," and then, in the shape of the Episcopal clergy, shut him up for twelve years in Bedford gaol. All this is gone for ever. But let us not rejoice prematurely: the old giant is still alive. He may be seen in many shapes, on all sides, and with many voices. "The spirit of burning and the spirit of judgment" have not, as some lament, altogether departed either from Churchmen or from Nonconformists. But his joints are very stiff and crazy; and when on this day the clergy and the magistrates of Bedford are seen rejoicing in common with their Dissenting brethren, at the inauguration of a memorial of him who once suffered at the hands of all their spiritual forefathers, it is a proof that the world has at least, in this respect, become a little more Christian, because a little more charitable and a little more enlightened—a little more capable of seeing the inward good behind outward differences.

An excellent and laborious Nonconformist, who devoted his life to the elucidation of the times and works of Bunyan, describes, with just indignation, the persecuting law of Charles II., under which John Bunyan was imprisoned, and he then adds, "This is now the law of the land we live in." No, my good Nonconformist brother, no, thank God! it is not now, nor has for many a long year, been in force amongst us. In the very year in which John Bunyan died, that Revolution took place to which, when compared with all the numerous revolutions which have since swept over other countries, may be well accorded the good old name "Glorious," and of which one of the most glorious fruits was the Toleration Act, by which such cruelties and follies as the Conventicle and Five Mile Acts became thenceforth and for ever impossible. That Act was, no doubt, only the first imperfect beginning; we have still, even now, all of us much to learn in this respect. But we have gained something; and this day is another pledge of the victory of the Christian faith, another nail knocked into the coffin of our ancient enemy. It required a union of many forces to effect the change. If it was Barlow, Bishop of Lincoln, that befriended John Bunyan in prison, it was Whitehead, the Quaker, whom, in his earlier days, Bunyan regarded as a heathen and an outcast, that opened for him the doors of Bedford gaol; and those doors were kept open by the wise King William III., by the Whig statesmen and Whig prelates of the day, and not least, by the great house of Russell, who, having protected the oppressed Nonconformists in the days of their trial, have in each succeeding generation opened the gates of the prison-house of prejudice and intolerance wider and wider still. Let it be our endeavour to see that they are not closed again either in Bedford or anywhere else.

4. Thus much I have felt constrained to say by the circumstances, local, ecclesiastical, and political, of this celebration. But I now enter on those points for which chiefly, no doubt, I have been asked to address you, and from which alone this monument has acquired its national importance. The hero of Elstow was great, the preacher in the Baptist meeting-house of Bedford was greater, but, beyond all comparison, greater was the dear teacher of the childhood of each of us, the creator of those characters whose names and faces are familiar to the whole world, the author of the "Pilgrim's Progress." And when I speak to you of Bunyan in this his world-wide aspect, I speak to you no longer as a stranger to the men of Bedford, but as an Englishman to Englishmen; no longer as a Churchman to Dissenters, but as a Christian to Christians, and as a man to men throughout the world. In the "Pilgrim's Progress" we have his best self—as superior to his own inferior self as to his contemporaries. It is one of the peculiar delights of that charming volume that when we open it all questions of Conformity or Nonconformity, of Baptists or Pædobaptists, even of Catholic and Protestant, are left far behind. It is one of the few books which act as a religious bond to the whole of English Christendom. It is, perhaps, with six others, and equally with any of those six, the book which, after the English Bible, has contributed to the common religious culture of the Anglo-Saxon race. It is one of the few books, perhaps almost the only English book, which has succeeded in identifying religious instruction with entertainment and

amusement both of old and young. It is one of the few books which has struck a chord which vibrates alike amongst the humblest peasants and amongst the most fastidious critics.

Let us pause for an instant to reflect how great a boon is conferred upon a nation by one such uniting element. How deeply extended is the power of sympathy, and the force of argument, when the preacher or the teacher knows that he can enforce his appeal by a name which, like that of an apostle or evangelist, comes home as if with canonical weight to every one who hears him; by figures of speech which need only be touched in order to elicit an electric spark of understanding and satisfaction. And when we ask wherein this power consists, let me name three points.

First, it is because the "Pilgrim's Progress," as I have already indicated, is entirely catholic—that is, universal in its expression and its thoughts. I do not mean to say— it would be an exaggeration—that it contains no sentiments distasteful to this or that section of Christians, that it has not a certain tinge of the Calvinist or the Puritan. But what is remarkable is that this peculiar colour is so very slight. We know what was Bunyan's own passionate desire on this point. "I would be," he says, "as I hope I am, 'a Christian,' but as for those factious titles of Anabaptist, Independent, Presbyterian, or the like, I conclude that they come neither from Jerusalem nor Antioch, but from hell or Babylon." It was this universal charity that he expressed in his last sermon, "Dost thou see a soul that has the image of God in him? Love him, love him. This man and I must go to heaven one day. Love one another, and do good for one another." It was this discriminating forbearance that he expressed in his account of the Interpreter's Garden. "Behold," he says, "the flowers are diverse in stature, in quality, in colour, in smell, and in virtue; and some are better than some; also where the gardener has set them there they stand and quarrel not with one another." There is no compromise in his words, there is no faltering in his convictions; but his love and admiration are reserved on the whole for that which all good men love, and his detestation on the whole is reserved for that which all good men detest. And if I may for a moment enter into detail, even in the very forms of his narrative we find something as universal as his doctrine. Protestant, Puritan, Calvinist as he was, yet he did not fear to take the framework of his story and the figures of his drama from the old mediæval Church, and the illustrations in which the modern editions of his book abound give us the pilgrim with his pilgrim's hat, the wayside cross, the crusading knight with his red-cross shield, the winged angels at the Celestial Gate, as naturally and as gracefully as though it had been a story from the " Golden Legend," or from the favourite romance of his early boyhood, " Sir Bevis of Southampton." Such a combination of Protestant ideas with Catholic forms had never been seen before, perhaps never since ; it is in itself a union of Christendom in the best sense, to which neither Catholic nor Protestant, neither Churchman nor Nonconformist, can possibly demur. The form, the substance, the tendency of the " Pilgrim's Progress" in these respects may be called latitudinarian, but it is a latitudinarianism which was an indispensable condition for its influence throughout the world. By it, as has been well said by an admirable living authority learned in all the learning of the Nonconformists, John Bunyan became the teacher, not of any particular sect, but of the universal Church.

Secondly, this wonderful book, with all its freedom, is never profane ; with all its devotion, is rarely fanatical ; with all its homeliness, is never vulgar. In other words, it is a work of pure art and true genius, and wherever these are we mount at once into a freer and loftier air. Bunyan was in this sense the Burns of England. On the tinker of Bedfordshire, as on the ploughman of Ayrshire, the heavenly fire had been breathed which transformed the common clay and made him a poet, a philosopher—may we not say a gentleman and a nobleman in spite of himself. "If you were to polish the style," says Coleridge, " you would destroy the reality of the vision." He dared (and it was, for one of his straitened school and scanty culture, an act of immense daring) to communicate his religious teaching in the form of fiction, dream, poetry. It is one of the most striking proofs of the superiority of literature over polemics, of poetry over prose, as a messenger of heavenly truth. " I have been better entertained and more informed," says Dean Swift, " by a few pages of the 'Pilgrim's Progress' than by a long discourse on the will and the intellect." "I have," says Arnold, "always been struck by its piety. I am now equally struck, and even more, by its profound wisdom." It might perhaps have been thought that Bunyan, with his rough and imperfect education, must have erred—as it may be he has sometimes erred—in defective appreciation of virtues and weaknesses not his own; but one prevailing characteristic of his work is the breadth and depth of his intellectual insight. For the sincere tremors of poor Mrs. Much-afraid he has as good a word of consolation as he has for the ardent aspirations of Faithful and Hopeful. For the dogmatic nonsense of Talkative he has a word of rebuke as strong as he has for the gloomy dungeons of Doubting Castle; and for the treasures of the past he has a feeling as tender and as pervasive as if he had been brought up in the cloisters of Oxford or Westminster Abbey.

When (if I may for a moment speak of myself) in early youth I lighted on the passage where the Pilgrim is taken to the House Beautiful to see "the pedigree of the Ancient of Days, and the rarities and histories of that place, both ancient and modern," I determined that if ever the time should arrive when I should become a professor of ecclesiastical history, these should be the opening words in which I would describe the treasures of that magnificent storehouse. Accordingly when, many years after, it so fell out, I could find no better mode of beginning my course at Oxford than by redeeming that early pledge; and when the course came to an end, and I wished to draw a picture of the prospects yet reserved for the future of Christendom, I found again that the best words I could supply were those in which, on leaving the Beautiful house, Christian was shown in the distance the view of the Delectable Mountains, "which, they said, would add to his comfort because they were nearer to the desired haven." What was my own experience in one special branch of knowledge may also be the experience of many others. And for the nation at large, all who appreciate the difficult necessity of refining the atmosphere and cultivating the taste of the uneducated and the half-educated may be thankful that in this instance there is a well of English language and of Christian thought, pure and undefiled, at which the least instructed and the best instructed may alike come to quench their mental thirst, and to refresh their intellectual labours. On no other occasion could such a rustic assemblage have been seen taking part in the glorification of a literary work as we have witnessed this day in Bedford. That is a true education of the people—an education which we know not perhaps whether to call denominational or undenominational, but which is truly national, truly Christian, truly divine.

Lastly, there is the practical, homely, energetic insight into the heart of man, and the spiritual needs of human nature, which make his picture of the Pilgrim's heavenward road a living drama, not a dead disquisition, a thing to be imitated, not merely to be read. Look at John Bunyan himself as he stands before you, whether in the description of his own contemporaries or in the image now so skilfully carved amongst you by the hand of the sculptor. As surely as he walked your streets with his lofty, stalwart form, "tall of stature, strong boned, with sparkling eyes, wearing his hair on his upper lip after the old British fashion, his hair reddish, but in his latter days sprinkled with grey, his nose well cut, his mouth moderately large, his forehead something high, and his habit always plain and modest;" as surely also as he was known amongst his neighbours as "in countenance of a stern and rough temper, but in his conversation mild and affable, not given to loquacity unless occasion required it, observing never to boast of himself, but rather seeming low in his own eyes, and submitting himself to the judgment of others; abhorring lying and swearing, being just in all that lay in his power to his word, not seeming to revenge injuries, but loving to reconcile differences and make friendship with all, with a sharp, quick eye, accomplished with an excellent discerning of person, being of good judgment and quick wit;" as surely as he so seemed when he was alive, as surely as he was one of yourselves, a "man of the people," as you heard at St. Peter's Green this morning, a man of the people of England and the people of Bedford—so surely is the pilgrimage which he described the pilgrimage of every one amongst us, so surely are the combinations of the neighbours, the friends, the enemies whom he saw in his dream the same as we see in our actual lives. You and I, as well as he, have met with Mr. By-ends, and Mr. Facing-both-ways, and Mr. Talkative. Some of us, perhaps, may have seen Mr. Nogood and Mr. Liveloose, Mr. Hatelight and Mr. Implacable. All of us have at times been like Mr. Ready-to-halt, Mr. Feeblemind, and Faintheart, and Noheart, and Slowpace, and Shortwind, and Sleepyhead, and "the young woman whose name was Dull." All of us need to be cheered by the help of Greatheart, and Standfast, and Valiant for the Truth, and good old Honest. Some of us have been in Doubting Castle, some in the Slough of Despond; some have experienced the temptations of Vanity Fair; all of us have to climb the Hill Difficulty, all of us need to be instructed by the Interpreter in the House Beautiful; all of us bear the same burden; all of us need the same armour in our fight with Apollyon; all of us have to pass through the wicket gate, all of us have to pass through the dark river; and for all of us (if God so will) there wait the Shining Ones at the gates of the Celestial City, "which, when we see, we wish ourselves amongst them."

Dean Stanley, the Church, and Bunyan.

BY THE RIGHT HON. EARL COWPER, K.G.,
Lord Lieutenant of Bedfordshire.

In some respects I feel myself rather unfortunate in coming after the Dean of Westminster; but in one respect this is a time of all others for me to say anything which I wish to say; for the feeling that is uppermost in my own mind at this moment must be uppermost in all your minds, and it is one of intense gratitude to the Dean of Westminster for having come down here to-day to take part in the proceedings. He has told you that the only, or almost the only, claim of the town of Bedford to a world-wide reputation is the name of John Bunyan; and that is, of course, quite true; but I may perhaps say with equal truth—though we may expect to hear other able and eloquent discourses—that if not the only, yet the

chief claim of this gathering to universal fame will be the
fact that the Dean of Westminster has given us that
admirable and forcible address on the great subject of this
gathering. Nobody can feel more how exhaustive that
speech was than I do at this moment, who have to follow
him. I had intended to speak of the house of Russell, and
their services in the cause of liberty and other great
causes; but that ground has been cut from under my feet.
For a long time I did not think I should speak at all here
to-day, but as soon as I knew that I should be expected to
do so, I began to consider that I might talk of the scenes
of Bunyan's youth around us, which you see every day,
and I very often; but I find these much more graphically
described by a stranger, who comes from London, than
they could be even by those who have been familiar with
them all their lives. On one or two previous occasions I have met the Dean of Westminster at local meetings, and, strange to say, I always find he picks out something either in local archæology or history on which he
knows more than even the inhabitants themselves. It is
to me as a Bedford man, holding the position of Lord-
Lieutenant of this county, a great gratification to be present to-day. We all know how intimately the town of
Bedford is associated with the great name of John
Bunyan; we know that people of all countries, from
America particularly, make pilgrimages to this neighbourhood, to see the birth-place and dwelling-place of John
Bunyan, in the same way as they do to Stratford-on-
Avon, to see the home of Shakespeare; and now that that
statue is put up, what strikes us more than anything else
is why on earth it should not have been thought of before.
In Stratford-on-Avon every corner of every street has a
memorial of some sort to the memory of Shakespeare, but
we have had nothing till now. The defect has now
been remedied, and remedied by one to whom we shall
all be eternally grateful—the Duke of Bedford. There
is nobody by whom we feel the gift could be more
fittingly made than by him. I am glad that the
chief part to-day has been taken by a minister of the
Church of England. The history of John Bunyan is
one which must fill every member of the Church with
feelings of reproach and of grief, when we consider what

his life was, and what intolerance was manifested with regard to him. This would not happen now, and I think we may feel that if John Bunyan had lived in our days his statue would not have been placed with his back to the Church, as it now is, but with his face to it, even though, like many other good men, he might have declined to enter it. I have been connected with the neighbourhood of Bedford for some time, and I think everybody who knows the town will agree with me that this is a place in which the Protestants of all denominations are closely united. I am chairman of a school in this neighbourhood founded on a broad Protestant foundation, and, though we have had our difficulties, like every one else, we have never had a single difficulty from causes connected with religion. All I can say is, the difficulties which people might imagine in such a case have never arisen here. All have worked well together, and that has shown me that the feeling which pervades Bedford is a desire to sink our differences, and to unite in furthering those great truths in which we agree. I cannot but express a hope that the statue which has been this day unveiled may long continue in this town. I am glad that a memorial of the great man has at last been erected, and I am glad that it has been erected by the Duke of Bedford.

Bunyan and Religious Liberty.

BY THE REV. W. BROCK, D.D.

My lords, ladies, and gentlemen, I thank the **Dean of Westminster** from my heart for his paper, and especially for that portion in which he spoke so kindly of his Nonconformist brethren. Bunyan, I take it, was one of the sowers of seed, the harvest of which we **are** reaping now, and our children will go on to reap in **days yet to come.** The principle which was in vogue in **his time** was that all religious thought and practice should be accordant with the established forms. Bunyan took up with the opposite principle, and whilst he did not like the forms he disliked them yet more thoroughly as the **interference** of the civil power with **the freedom of** religious thought and practice, and so he determined that he would act contrary to them. But he **was in** difficulties, for of all the loyal subjects of this realm, **John** Bunyan was about the most loyal. He ranked himself among those old-fashioned folk who delighted to fear **God** and honour the King, even when that **King was** Charles II. What, then, could one so loyal do when the authorities required him to conform his **religious thought** and practice to the established forms? **He went on to** judge for himself, and to act for himself; **not that it was** the slightest pleasure to him to be **in** opposition to **the** magistrate, but when it **became** a matter of disobeying the magistrate or disobeying God, **then his course was** clear. Alien to his habits and tendencies altogether were those of the noisy, boisterous demagogue, who would be going about instigating sedition and stirring up strife. He was, to all intents and purposes, a most loyal citizen, determined, as far as ever he could, that he would obey the law; but in regard to this matter of religious **thought and** practice, he insisted upon it that a man must be free; for no human law had any right whatever to interfere, and no **human law was** binding in the slightest degree, in regard to **a** man's apprehension of God or behaviour of himself towards God. If human law came to him proffering emoluments and honour touching matters that were religious, he felt himself under obligation to decline both the emolument and the honour; and if the human law came and threatened him with pains and penalties, he thought it right to incur them all, and thus thinking and thus resolving, by-and-by he did publicly take up with the practice of free prayer, in contradistinction from the Liturgy, and, deeming it his duty to preach the Gospel, he determined that he would preach it wheresoever and whensoever he could. The opportunities were not very frequent, unless he would disguise himself; and some of you recollect how graphically Lord Macaulay describes the disguising. Unless he disguised himself, and preached at dead of night, and in secluded places, opportunities for preaching were but few. But Bunyan thoroughly disliked disguise in all forms and shapes. It was most foreign to his nature, and he would not consent to be dressed up any more. What he did he resolved to do openly, in the face of day, in the cause of his Divine Master; and so one day there was an arrangement made that he should preach at Samsell. He was told that if he did so the constable would be upon his track, and he would certainly be taken up; and there is not a more instructive passage in all his writings than that in which he tells us of the exercise of his mind in that very matter. For example, he says—" God has chosen me to go on this forlorn hope of preaching His blessed Gospel in this country; and I should discourage those who are coming after me if I should be afraid and fly. Besides, the world would take occasion from my cowardliness to blaspheme the Gospel; so I must needs go and preach." Accordingly, when the time came, he was found at his post at Samsell. If so be the magistrate would enforce the law in regard to preaching and religious worship it must be so. He would obey the magistrate actively if he could, and if not he would passively obey by enduring the penalty, whatever that penalty may be. So he went, and the service began. There was the due attention to psalmody, and prayer, and the reading of God's Word; and then there came the announcement of his text, " Dost thou believe on the Son of God?" In walked a constable with his warrant for the arrest of John Bunyan there and then. The congregation broke up, of course, and he was taken into custody forthwith. Next day he was taken before the magistrate, and then ensued one of the most singular dialogues or discussions one has ever read. You remember that Bunyan was insisting upon it that he had a right to preach, and the justice asked, "What right has a tinker to preach?" "Well," Bunyan said, "as a tinker he has no right, but then as a man of whom the tinker is made up he has a right, or should have a right, and presuming that he has the physical and intellectual and spiritual qualifications he certainly has the right. In case the Church to which he belongs recognises the right, all the better; but *that* it is which constitutes his right, that he is a faithful man, and able to teach others also." "Then you won't give up your preaching?" said the justice. "Never," replied the tinker; "as a man has received the gift so let him minister according to the ability which God has given to him. If you must enforce your human law against what I believe to be Divine law, be it so. I would obey you actively if I could; as I cannot do that, I am ready to obey you passively by submitting to the penalty, even if it should be death itself." And believing that he had ability given to him, he insisted upon it that he was under no obligation to the magistrate, but under the highest obligation to God to go and exercise that ability forthwith. Well, the dialogue went on, and here and there was still more curious, but the end of it was, as you know, that he was committed to gaol—that gaol which, I suppose, he had in his eye as the den, as was intimated just now by the Dean. Some excitement was created, and it was very generally known that he was sent to gaol on that particular account. Efforts were made by more than one person of consideration to get him to change his mind, and to renounce his determination to preach. They talked to him about the gaol and its irksomeness to a man of 32, in the full vigour of life and health, accustomed to the open air and open country. He knew that better than they did. It was suffering, but then it was "suffering for conscience' sake," and he determined that he would bear it even unto the end, for he would not give up. You remember the strong expression which he used on one occasion, when he was defending the practice of certain Christian brethren. Being pressed and pressed again, he became, I suppose, a little resentful, and he said, "The moss shall grow on my eyebrows before I give up that principle." Well, he went on, thus pertinaciously adhering to his determination in this matter. For six years he never left that den. We have it, I believe, on conclusive evidence that the first six years were very severe, and some of the passages in his writings indicative of his feelings at that time, and of the fact originating the feelings, will a little dissipate the opinion I have heard expressed that after all there was not much severity in his imprisonment. His imprisonment was so severe that he was pressed out of measure, above strength, so that sometimes he despaired even of life. During the second six years there was a moderation. He made friends with the gaoler. I believe he made friends with everybody. He was one of the most pleasant, agreeable, neighbourly men the world ever saw. By-and-by, in the providence of God, deliverance came. He was released, and came out of gaol, but was molested frequently after that, and had to stand up for liberties and rights, and stand up he did. He never shirked, he never shrank from doing his duty in that direction, and he left every one of those liberties unbetrayed, and all those rights uncompromised. And in doing all that he was sowing the seed of which we are reaping the harvest to-day. Who would go and disturb a meeting at Samsell now, I should like to know? Who would set the constable or the magistrate going now in regard to the freedom of religious practice or religious thought? Let a man be an honest, upright, straightforward citizen and neighbour; let him live a quiet and peaceful life in all honesty and godliness, not violating promises which he has deliberately made, nor betraying trusts which have been committed to his care, and he may go and pray in free prayer anywhere, and he may go and preach in City Temples or in Metropolitan Tabernacles, or Agricultural Halls, or in country barns. Why, if Bunyan could come back, he might preach at Cotton End in the morning, at Elstow in the afternoon, and at Bedford at night, and anywhere else he liked. He would be consigned to no den; not because he would have come over to the magistrates' opinion, but because the magistrates have come over to his. Persecuting is almost out of fashion and out of date, though, as our friend the Dean intimated, we may be a little premature in our joy in that matter. Still, it is going rapidly out of fashion, as well as out of date, and the harvest which we are now reaping should make us thankful beyond all expression. Our freedom is not an **accident**; it is a consequence and it is a result. If those predecessors of ours had ingloriously succumbed to the intolerance to which they were subjected, that intolerance **would** have been in the ascendant to-day; and it is to **Milton's** plea for unlicensed printing, and to Bunyan's practice of unlicensed preaching, and, in justice **let** me add, to Jeremy Taylor's assertion of the liberty of prophesying, that our privileges are, under God, to be ascribed now. Well, then, let the cry and **the** watchword be the maintenance of those principles; **no** revocation of Acts of Emancipation; no re-enactment, even by implication, of Test or Corporation Acts; **no** submission **of** the people's privileges either to the sacerdotal pretensions of the priest—bad enough as they are—or to the imperious **dictation of** the doctrinaire, which I suspect would be **found to** be a good deal worse. Let there be no withdrawal from any reputable citizen of any privilege whatsoever which we ourselves enjoy, and touching these matters of religious thought and religious practice, let it be equality for us all, and ascendancy **for** none. I cannot help making a passing allusion to-day to a nobleman whose attachment to our constitutional **freedom** led him to a most illustrious and a right venerable end. All honour to Lord William Russell, whose **martyrdom** in those fields of Lincoln's Inn gave such a momentum, such an immense impulse to our country's determination to bring political and ecclesiastical tyranny to the dust. The plebeian of Elstow did his part heroically; the patrician of Woburn Abbey did his heroically, and I may say with more solemnity still, for under the axe of the executioner he maintained that the individual and the nation should be free. All honour to Lord William Russell, and **equal** honour to his brave and high-minded lady, one of the **purest and** the saintliest and the perfectest helpmeets that **God ever** gave to man. I could **not** help the allusion, gathered **as we are to-day at** the inauguration of **a** statue of John Bunyan, the generous and spontaneous **gift of** his Grace the Duke of Bedford. The associations **of the** house of Russell with our nation's freedom are manifold and full of interest. We have another added to the rest of them to-day, one of the most graceful and grateful and congenial of them all; and it stands there, and will stand, I hope, as long as Bedford shall remain, an indication of what the house of Russell is in continuance, even as it has been in so many times that are past, and as I hope it will be to the very end of time.

At the Mayor's dinner in the evening Dr. Brock, in responding to the toast of "The Bishop of the Diocese, and other Ministers of Religion," said he believed if John Bunyan were at that gathering he would be quite at home in responding to the toast, as, according to Mr. Offor, he was made Chaplain to the Lord Mayor of London, in token of the civic admiration and respect. This was not generally known. No doubt Bunyan did the duties of his chaplaincy very well indeed, those which were connected with the hospitalities of the Mansion House among the rest. He (Dr. Brock) thanked them for having connected his name with the toast. Not long ago he was in a company nearly as large and august as this, when one of the bishops said that although an effort had been made some two centuries ago to get rid of the Church of England, it was evident that the people would still have it. He then ventured to say that the country would evidently have Nonconformity as well. That one moiety of the community preferred to worship in the church was not to be denied; but that the other moiety preferred to worship in the meeting-house was safely to be affirmed. The reverend gentleman who preceded him, and he himself, were equally the objects of the country's choice. They could all, however, meet in goodwill. One man's way was not another man's—there was a difference of gifts and a variety of operations, but then all could labour with one object in their view: exhorting their several congregations to honour all men, to love the brotherhood, to serve God, and honour the Queen.

The Literary Genius of John Bunyan.

BY THE REV. HENRY ALLON, D.D.

We recognise to-day a great deal more than the genius of John Bunyan. If one were looking out for a theme for moralising, the most suggestive is, that we who have gathered together to-day thus combine to recognise it. To right-hearted men few things could be more grateful than such an exorcism of the spirit of the past, or a better augury for the spirit of the future. It is not, I think, any violation of the noble catholicity of feeling which has brought us here; nor will it, I trust, be invidiously construed, that such a recognition of the vast change in religious and ecclesiastical feeling which this inauguration marks should fall from Nonconformist lips. I am sure that there is no one here that hails it with more of hearty, thankful gladness, than my noble-hearted friend, Dean Stanley, whose presence here is only one of many expressions of a catholic recognition of good in all churches and classes of men. In him, however, it is not so much a dictate of Christian duty as it is a necessary sympathy, the essential feeling of a noble nature, to which intolerance and assumption are simply impossible. And with this feeling thousands of English Episcopalians are in sympathy; the donation of this statue of John Bunyan by the Duke of Bedford is only a representative expression of it. To be delivered from the spirit of intolerance is really a greater salvation than to be delivered from its endurance. And this salvation has, I think, been experienced by us all. I am not sure that the proud resentment of the Nonconformist has not been often as impracticable and repellant as the scornful oppression of his opponent. Religious persecution has this evil also to answer for, that it sours the sweet charities of Christian hearts, hardens mere preferences into matters of conscience, and makes endurance a pride. It is a great and gracious progress of Christian charity in our entire national life that we celebrate; and in our progress towards it it is doubtful on which side the grace has been greatest. I neither expect nor desire that religious parties in England will ever all subscribe the same creeds or be gathered into one ecclesiastical body. This could be only at the cost, either of God's great law of diversity in human nature, or of moral sincerity in the expression of it. But this inauguration, I think, expresses the much higher grace of a manly recognition, a generous charity, and a true religious brotherhood in the presence of such diversities. Let us thank God that we have lived to see the day when good men are so free from the blind passion of religious party as to recognise good in all parties, and are fearless enough openly to do homage to it: when they can maintain and debate their differences without the immolation as a war-sacrifice of the sweet charities of life, and without injuring in any way the delicate sensitiveness of brotherly affection.

Of all the retrospective imaginations of to-day, the most impossible is, that the anticipation of such a celebration should have occurred to Bunyan himself. Bunyan was greatest when he was dreaming; but his wildest dreams could not have surmised this day, when the bi-centenary of his release from prison would be celebrated by the inauguration of a public statue to himself in his own town of Bedford; the gift of a descendant of the Earl of Bedford, of whom perhaps he had heard with distant awe, elevated to the highest rank of the English peerage, and, can we doubt, representing the admiring appreciation of our gracious and noble-hearted Sovereign;* consecrated by a picturesque and eloquent eulogy, such as can fall from no other lips, from one of the most accomplished dignitaries of the very Church in whose name he was persecuted; presided over by the mayor, himself not a Nonconformist; and hailed by his fellow townsmen as their most illustrious citizen. And that by a singular coincidence, a eulogistic biography of him should at the same time be published by the Vicar of Elstow, of all places in the world, the village in the church of which he had so morbidly and madly done

---

* When Queen Victoria stood sponsor at the baptism of the eldest son of the Prince of Wales, she presented to her grandchild a silver statuette of the late Prince Consort in the character of "Christian" in the "Pilgrim's Progress." Thus Her Majesty was really before the Duke of Bedford in doing honour to John Bunyan.—ED.

his bell-ringing, on the green of which he had on Sunday evenings played at pitch and toss, and in the streets of which, with unimaginable dreamings of things human and Divine, he had plied his tinker's craft. Of all the vicissitudes of reputation which Time the avenger brings, this is surely the most romantic, unless, indeed, it be that of the butcher boy of Stratford-on-Avon charged as a deer-stealer before Sir Thomas Lucy, then consecrating his native town as the most illustrious of the literary shrines of the world, at which pilgrims from every part of the civilised world are glad to do homage.

One has only to think of Bunyan in the Sessions' House at Bedford indicted before Justice Keeling, the charge being, "That John Bunyan, of the town of Bedford, labourer, hath devilishly and pertinaciously abstained from coming to church to hear Divine service, and is a common upholder of several unlawful meetings and conventicles, to the great disturbance of the good subjects of this kingdom;" and of the unanswerable ruling of the erudite judge that the Book of Common Prayer had existed "ever since the apostles' times;" and of his equally notable paraphrase of Bunyan's Scriptural justification of his preaching, "As every man hath received the gift so he is to minister the same to another;" "Just so," replied the judge, "as every one hath received a trade so let him follow it. If any man hath received the gift of tinkering, as thou hast done, let him follow his tinkering." Poor Justice Keeling, a gift of tinkering was all that was given him to see in John Bunyan:—and then the sentence of three months' imprisonment and the warning that accompanied it. "If you do not then submit to go to church to hear Divine service, and leave your preaching, you must be banished the realm; and if, after such day as shall be appointed you to be gone, you shall be found in this realm . . . . you must stretch by the neck for it, I tell you plainly." Bunyan was not docile—"If you let me out to-day, I will preach again to-morrow." Perhaps a certain apostolic precedent, when a similar coercion was attempted by the Jewish Sanhedrim, was responsible for this blunt intractableness. Hence his three months' imprisonment was extended to twelve years. At first it was strict and severe, but in the latter part of it greatly relaxed. To his honour be it spoken, Barlow, the Bishop of the diocese, is said to have interceded for Bunyan; although, on the other hand, it is said that certain bishops in London were so angry when they heard of the relaxation, that they sent down an officer to inquire. Under some mysterious inspiration, Bunyan, who had received permission to spend that night with his family, was impelled to return to prison. The gaoler grumbled at having to admit him at so untimely an hour. Soon after, the officer arrived, and demanded to see Bunyan, and departed satisfied: thus the gaoler escaped. "Well," said he to his prisoner, "you may go out again just as you think proper, for you know when to return better than I can tell you." Bunyan tells us that he availed himself of his liberty to follow his wonted course of preaching and exhorting the people "to be steadfast in the faith of Jesus Christ, and to take heed that they touched not the Book of Common Prayer." Also that he "did go at Christmas to London." He seems to have been somewhat disappointed at the leniency with which he was treated. He expected to have been "roundly dealt withal," and had specially studied Foxe's "Book of Martyrs" in order to fortify his martyr-spirit. He was not even called up at the November sessions of 1661, although he had hoped that at least his name would have appeared in the calendar "among the felons." No doubt he wished to testify before the judges. There he remained until 1672 "in the common gaol for our county of Bedford," as it is described in the order for his release under Charles II. It was not, therefore, the gaol on the bridge, which has so long claimed the traditional honour. From prison he went to the more regular discharge of his duties as pastor of the Baptist congregation in Bedford, to which office he had been elected during the eleventh year of his imprisonment. Such things were when Bunyan lived, and to-day the name of John Bunyan is a household word throughout the world; and we are here doing honour to ourselves more than to him—for this homage shows that we have attained to a higher intellectual appreciation, a nobler religious sympathy. Homage to genius or to goodness is the expression of all that is best in a man. The greater the excellency of any work of the Creator, the greater the reverence that it demands. Defect of reverence is defect in that part of our nature which renders its supreme worship to the Creator Himself. The refusal of homage to any genuine form of greatness is simply the indication of our own little incapacity; for power of reverence is the highest quality of noble natures.

Perhaps the great lesson of the celebration of to-day is the persistence and imperishableness of true genius. Thanks to the divine art of printing, a book once given to the world is well-nigh an imperishable possession. Manuscripts often perished—sometimes they were not even copied; through accident or design it was comparatively easy to destroy them. How much the world has lost by the intolerance of religious passion we can never know. We should have known a great deal more about Christianity, and perhaps have been spared generations of misconception and blundering, had its too zealous champions spared the writings of its antagonists. It is almost impossible to kill a printed book. It can perish only by its own lack of vitality. However obscure its origin, however vigilant and implacable its foes, it finds its way to unsuspected places. There it bides its time, while contemporary passions rage, while even greater men than Justice Keeling are less excusably blind, and see in the John Bunyan of their day only a tinker fit for a gaol, and in its Defoe only a scribbler fit for a pillory. The quiet book remains, and if the divine mark of genius is upon it, it will be again and again brought up for judgment; and when, sooner or later, fierce passion has subsided, and prejudice is exorcised, so that a just judgment can be formed, it will be "crowned" in that Academy of Literature which neither Legislature nor Church can control. No power either of tyranny or of persecution can hinder a "Pilgrim's Progress" or a "Robinson Crusoe" from becoming the delight of nursery and schoolroom, the interpreter of life to all who are perplexed with its problems, and the practical guide and solace of all who need counsel and sympathy.

The change in literary appreciation which is indicated by the honour done to Bunyan is very remarkable. Clearly, literary criticism moves now in a freer atmosphere, and literary judgments are formed with a juster taste. A broader and more genuine catholicity of literary appreciation has been attained. The creator of a new type in literature does not wait long for just recognition; a moment of puzzled wonder, a second moment of critical pedantry, and the appreciation is general, generous, and jubilant. No Keats or Wordsworth could, now-a-days, be killed, or for half a generation arrested in his progress to fame, by the petulant "this will never do" of an arbitrary critic.

Like the far transcendant creations of Shakespeare, the "Pilgrim's Progress" was a revolt of imperial genius against the modes and regulations of literary pedantry. It was an appeal to human nature; and yet it was long before its great qualities, as a new type of literature, were fully recognised. It soon became popular among the middle and lower classes. Eight editions were published within thirty years; but for more than a century it was the Pariah of literary genius. It was taken for granted that its appeal was only to the fanatical vulgarity of the conventicle. Every edition was printed for only plebeian readers. Coarse paper, small type, rude engravings, were its only embodiment. Literary judgments disparaged it, art disregarded it. And yet the latent qualities of it waited for its recognition as the greatest of religious allegories and the mother of English fiction. Dr. Johnson, indeed, who rarely read through a book, paid it the high compliment of wishing it longer. But Dr. Young saw in it nothing to distinguish it from the dreary prolixity, the leaden liveliness, of a French romance of 6,000 pages, by D'Urfe —then very popular, now utterly forgotten—and which it would be an adequate test of modern sanity to read at all. Other high literary authorities classified it with "Jack the Giant-Killer"—not so bad a comparison after all; for a lengthened religious allegory that can charm juvenile readers more than "Jack the Giant-Killer" must possess high qualities. Even Cowper, whose natural genius and religious sympathies alike qualified him for appreciating it, is somewhat timid in his praise, and did not venture to name so rude a prophet of the conventicle—

> "I name thee not, lest so despised a name
> Should move a sneer at thy deserved fame,
> Ingenious dreamer! in whose well-told tale,
> Sweet fiction and sweet truth alike prevail;
> Whose humorous vein, strong sense, and simple style
> May teach the gayest, make the gravest smile;
> Witty and well employed, and, like thy Lord,
> Speaking in parables His slightest word."—*Tirocinium.*

The "inconsiderable generation" of Bunyan was the great stumbling-block. Genius could not be the dower of an illiterate tinker; nor could its creations be demeaned to such a Puritan embodiment; nor could the rude Amos of a Baptist meeting-house be conceived of as God's prophet. To Southey and Macaulay belong the honour of placing Bunyan in his true niche in the Pantheon of literature. Even so just and dispassionate a critic as Henry Hallam is hesitating in his praise, and suggests a common rank, and that an inferior one, to the *spirituelle* and imaginative genius of Bunyan, and the realistic and somewhat earthly literary art of Defoe.

Genius is of no sect; it has intrinsic qualities which instinctively transcend all sectarianism. In spite of itself even, it soars and ranges above the jealous encampments and the fierce party strifes amid which it may accidentally work. It touches human life, and asserts its catholic affinities with all that is common in it. Milton, in the divine imagination of the "Paradise Lost," soars transcendantly above both his political republicanism and his religious Puritanism. "Robinson Crusoe" gives no indications of Defoe's vehement Nonconformity. Who from the "Pilgrim's Progress" could identify Bunyan's sect? May I, without violating this broad catholicity, traverse the charge of intellectual paucity and narrowness, sometimes urged against Puritans and Nonconformists, by reminding you that the author of our greatest English epic, the author of our greatest religious allegory, and the author of our most popular fiction, were all Puritans and Nonconformists? The claim to be the father of English romance, which has sometimes been preferred for Defoe, really pertains to Bunyan. Defoe may claim the parentage of a species, but Bunyan is the creator of the genus. Although intensely religious in purpose, character, and interest, the "Pilgrim's Progress" is the first English novel. As an allegory it had many predecessors —and has affinities with what in every age, and in various forms, has been a popular form of literature. The "Faerie Queen" is only the supreme form of it. But it is so much more than allegory that, in as absolute a sense as can be affirmed of any book, it may fairly claim to be a type of its own. If this element allies it with mediæval allegory, its dramatic history and its human passion and interest give it much more in common with the realistic character of modern fiction. Nor is it the less original because it is so largely drawn from the two great sources of religious inspiration—the Bible as our supreme revelation of theology, and the religious experiences of human nature. Into the grand mould of Bunyan's genius these two rich streams of material flow; the result is a creation of concrete forms in which all that is divinest in divine conception and teaching, and all that is noblest in the religious struggles and passions and realisations of human life, are embodied in imperishable truth, beauty, and grandeur. In the "Pilgrim's Progress" there is more of the Bible than there is in "Paradise Lost;" and, in the higher range of experience which it treats, more of human nature than there is in Shakespeare. It may be that in Bunyan power of dramatic representation was greater than the power of creative conception. And yet, one cannot help feeling that the moulding, combining, and colouring power of Bunyan are to the materials employed what the genius of the sculptor is to the pure marble and graceful model with which nature supplies him.

Like all creators Bunyan did not know what he did. He did not purpose a manufacture or a building, the completed plan of which has to be shaped before it is begun. He produced a living thing, developed from its germ, the germinant possibilities of which he did not suspect,—at first a faint suggestion, developed and shaped, filled in and perfected, by instinctive and half-conscious power, by quick-witted imagination, by intuitive touch; which seized on analogies and developed characteristics into typical embodiments, and casual incidents into normal conditions of action; and which, as a completed whole, in its epical unity, underlying truth, and artistic proportion and beauty, surprised no one so much as its author—if indeed he ever realised at all how great a thing he had done. We can well believe him when he says, "He wrote as if joy did make him write." It was not literary art, it was the natural instinct of genius beneath which the "Pilgrim's Progress" grew; which so unerringly relegated incidents to their proper place, and so fearlessly accepted circumstantial incongruities,—the death of Faithful, for instance, at Vanity Fair, in the middle of the ideal pilgrimage, and without crossing the river of death. But incongruities are not merely inevitable in an extended, diversified, and dramatic allegory—they are the legitimate liberties of genius, which boldly subordinates the letter to the spirit, the lower truth to the higher.

In creative genius Shakespeare stands supreme among men, and yet in the fearless freedom of his great spirit he did not hestitate to develop his grand creations out of the material of obscure chroniclers or Italian tale-writers. Handel again seized any musical ideas that lay ready to his hand. Bunyan was more spontaneous than either. He can scarcely be suspected of literary imitation or suggestion. It is doubtful whether the "Faerie Queen" was ever known to him. Assuredly the "Pilgrim's Progress" is as unlike it as common English life is unlike a Greek tragedy. Christian, and Faithful, and Greatheart are as remote from the frigid personifications around which Spenser grouped so much cold sublimity and distant goodness, as Shakespeare's Macbeth is from Holinshed's History of Scotland. Bunyan's bold personifications are exaggerated types, but they are full of human nature; diversified and novel, they interpret for us almost every experience and mood of religious life, just as the passionate expressions of David's Psalms do. We throb with sympathy and tremble with excitement; we melt to tears, and burn with ardours; every touch penetrates our human souls and interprets our most sacred experiences. Probably more tears of true and wholesome emotion have been shed over the "Pilgrim's Progress" than over any book ever written. While Spenser's personifications are mere lay figures, which command intellectual admiration and moral approval, Bunyan's characters are touched with emotion; in a marvellous way they blend abstract qualities with human sympathies, moral strength with gentle considerateness, rich, keen satire with unspeakable tenderness. Its daring imaginations are forgotten in the absorbing sense of reality. Its personages exist—a few rapid touches, and living men and women take us into their confidence, and identify themselves with our experiences. Bunyan is the Elijah of Puritanism, as tender as he is strong, as loving as he is fearless. We are excited as by family interests; we are edified more than by a thousand sermons. He touches all the springs of our souls—our penitence, our prayer, our holiness, our worship—and fills our sentiment of religion with its highest inspirations. We are ready to fight with Apollyon, to climb Hills Difficulty, to gaze upon Delectable Mountains, to rest in the Land of Beulah, and to wait with calm expectation until our summons shall come to pass over the river. We enter into the feeling with which the glorious dreamer saw those pilgrims enter who were "preferred before him"—the feeling which finds such perfect expression in the serene words of the close of the first dream; and that finds relief from the highly-wrought description of the Celestial City, by an inimitable touch of simple nature: "And after that they shut up the gates, which, when I had seen, I wished myself among them." And all this presented in vivid dramatic form, in a style that is vigorous, concise, and idiomatic, as simple as it is rich—which, like all things of pure nature, satisfies all tastes, charms all ears, and touches all hearts. Another proof, if such were wanting, that household words suffice for every form of literature, for all possibilities of passion.

I have spoken only of the "Pilgrim's Progress." It overshadows all Bunyan's other writings, just as "Robinson Crusoe" eclipses all those of Defoe. But for it the "Holy War" would be supreme after its kind. As a theological writer, Bunyan's vigorous thought, his epigrammatic sentences, and his passionate earnestness give him no mean place among the masculine thinkers and theologians who make its Puritan literature the glory of English Protestantism. As a preacher Bunyan had great gifts of oratory—not in Bedfordshire only, but in London, crowds filled to overflowing the largest building whenever it was known that he was going to preach. "I have seen," says an early biographer, "about twelve hundred at a morning lecture, by seven o'clock, on a working day, in the dark winter time. I also computed about three thousand that came to hear him one Lord's-day at London at a town's-end meeting-house, so that half were fain to go back again for want of room, and then himself was fain, at a back door, to be pulled almost over people to get upstairs to his pulpit." Dr. John Owen heard him preach, and when King Charles asked him how a man of his parts could endure the twaddle of a tinker, replied, "Could I possess the tinker's abilities, I would gladly relinquish all my learning." He rose to a wide and high esteem. As "Bishop Bunyan," he exercised the most honourable of all episcopates. He was the counsellor of thousands, the arbiter in disputes, and in the fulness of his fame and strength he sacrificed his life in seeking to mediate between an angry father and a disinherited son.

For the crown of his fame, and that which extends it to all classes and to all hearts, is the religious service to which his great gifts were consecrated. We have only to think of the maimed greatness, and of the partial and regretful homage which they command whose greatness has not been consecrated to goodness,—who have used great gifts to ridicule piety or corrupt morality. When genius devotes itself to the lofty service of religion and morality, all men do homage to it,—for it appeals to what is best in all, and commands their moral approval as well as their intellectual admiration. The broadest, the loftiest, the strongest throne of genius, is that which is rooted in the religious affections of men. There is no department of history or of life in which the old saying, as much the expression of natural laws as of God's promise, does not hold true, "Them that honour Me I will honour."

The Statue and the Time.

BY REV. J. BROWN, B.A.

I am indebted to the accident of my position rather than to any personal claim for the honour of moving the following resolution:—"That this meeting, representing the town of Bedford, and to some extent the country at large, desires to express its sense of the obligation under which his Grace the Duke of Bedford has placed the town and country by the munificent gift of the statue of John Bunyan, which has this day been unveiled." Sir, the resolution claims for this meeting a representative character, and rightly so. For if we look round we see in this great gathering gentlemen holding high official positions in the town and county, and we see also honoured friends from other places who really represent thousands more who would have been with us if they could, and who would have passed this resolution with all their hearts. Very varied classes of the community are with us to-day. Even the gaolers of the county gaol are here—they are here by a sort of prescriptive right, for I doubt not they are in the true succession of that old Bedford gaoler of 200 years ago who had charge of Bunyan, and who was one of the best friends Bunyan ever had. In fact, he was a much better man than he was a gaoler, and I hope that while the present warders are not less worthy as men they are more trustworthy as gaolers, and do not suffer their prisoners to sally forth on preaching excursions through the country. The erection of a statue to John Bunyan, in the town so closely associated with his life, his labours, and his sufferings, as has been said, is felt at once to be a thing so right and fitting, now that it is done, that one wonders it was not done generations ago. And yet, looking far afield upon the movements of the age, this was perhaps the most fitting time to bring this tribute of honour. And if it was to be done by any one man rather than by the nation, by no one could the tribute be so gracefully rendered as by the head of that house of Russell which derives its title from Bunyan's town, and which has always stood in the van of the movement for civil and religious liberty. This munificent act on the part of his Grace is in perfect keeping with the honourable traditions of his house. But more than that, it is an act of real personal homage. The wondrous story of the Dreamer was blended with the early associations of the Duke's childhood as with ours, and has stirred his heart as it has stirred the hearts of thousands more. This is not one of those condescending acts of patronage which make our manhood wince, but an honourable tribute honourably rendered to high creative genius, spiritual power, incorruptible integrity, and simplicity of life. We have seen to-day a new proof of the power of genius to go on inspiring the genius of others. The Pilgrim has already called forth the illustrations of Stothardt, Chas. Bennett, and others. And now in the bas-reliefs on the pedestal of the statue we have an independent contribution, and I think a real addition, to the art treasures of the country. The dwellers in the town and the pilgrims who come here from afar will have in those three vivid scenes a sort of speaking Bible. Right in front is a picture of that grim and unceasing battle with evil which ought to be the serious work of every man's life. On one side is the way to the wicket-gate, and on the other we seem to hear the salutation of the three shining ones by that cross which opens up the way of peace to sin-burdened men. And of the statue itself it is sufficient to say that it is a creation worthy of the sculptor's high reputation. There is about it that deep repose and that lofty spiritual ideality which we are in danger of losing in these busy, restless times, and which it is the province of the artist and the poet to preserve to us. It is an admirable conception, and as admirably placed. With leafy pleasant surroundings which give restfulness to the eye, the form yet stands out with due prominence and clearness of outline. It occurs, however, to the Lord-Lieutenant that standing where he does, Bunyan seems to be repeating his old offence in turning his back on the parish church. But I am sure our Church friends will judge him kindly. It is not an easy thing for men of his metal to face about at the word of command. He is only showing that he still belongs to those whom Dean Stanley has described as "Nonconforming members of the Church of England." The event of this day and the spirit in which it is being celebrated seem to bring somewhat nearer that other day for which some of us are longing when the first question asked of a man shall not be, "Is he a Churchman or a Dissenter?" but rather, "Is he a worthy man? does he live as he believes? has he any power by which he can serve the Commonwealth?" By the honour done to Bunyan it is admitted that a man may not be one whit less an Englishman because he comes to conclusions somewhat different from his neighbours on the deepest questions of his life. For if ever there was a true Englishman this man was one. His book is "a well of English, pure and undefiled," racy of the soil from which it sprang, vigorous with homely vigour, and steeped to the very heart in the genius of the people among whom it was born. But his book was not more thoroughly English than the spirit of his life. The man who when a warrant was out against him will not flee when he may, because, as he says, he ought to be as strong in deed as he had been in word; the man who when told that he might get out of trouble by merely saying a few words, replies that if they were such words as might be said with a good conscience he would say them, not else; the man who with or without reason began to suppose that his imprisonment might end on a scaffold was yet only concerned that he might not yield at last because it would be a shame to die with a pale face and tottering knees for such a cause as this; this man has surely as much of the real stuff of an Englishman about him as the men who won victory on the field of Waterloo, or quelled mutiny on the plains of India. Though (as the Dean of Westminster has told us) intolerance is not dead by any means, though for the present a separating line runs through much of our ecclesiastical and social life, we are yet only one nation, not two. The men who still think as Bunyan thought are as proud of the traditions of their country and as loyal to the lawful authority of the realm as the men who stand on the privileged ground of the Established Church. And I hope, nay, I am sure, we are nearing the time when ecclesiastical barriers between good men will fall, and when there shall be a true brotherhood of godly souls in this land,—a brotherhood which shall show itself by earnest work, shoulder to shoulder, in the great cause of God and man. Certainly this was the desire of the man whose memory we honour to-day. In that case before us are the Records of the Church with which Bunyan was connected for five-and-thirty years, and at the outset there are these memorable words:—"Now the principle upon which they thus entered into fellowship one with another, and upon which they did afterwards receive those that were added to their body and fellowship, was 'Faith in Christ and Holiness of Life,' without respect to this or that circumstance or opinion in outward and circumstantial things." On this truly catholic basis, and not on that of mere ecclesiastical organisation, may the Church of the future stand! I have pleasure, Mr. Mayor, in proposing the resolution.

Bunyan's Personal Pilgrimage.
BY THE REV. C. M. BIRRELL.

I.

The man whose memory has just been honoured by persons of the highest distinction for rank and learning tells us, with that manly humility which is equally remote from shame and pride, that he came "of a low and inconsiderable generation." Soon after the opening of that seventeenth century which was so fruitful of great events and great men, he might have been seen gambolling in rags about the cottage door of one of the poorest denizens of Elstow. His father was not indifferent to his instruction, for he sent him to school to obtain the rudiments of learning at a time when education was much less accessible to the working classes than it is now; and it was perhaps neither the father's nor the son's fault that what the little fellow acquired at that time he afterwards forgot "even almost utterly," for he was driven by poverty to bear a hand at the anvil instead of remaining at his horn-book until he had riveted his scanty attainments upon the memory.

As he emerged from his boyhood with vast and unregulated force of character, it is not surprising that he should have sought a sterner field of action than the village green. Born in 1628, the very year in which the Parliament passed the Bill of Rights, by the time he was seventeen the civil war was approaching its crisis. He makes but one allusion to the fact that he joined the army. It was a subject which, when all was over, he was willing to let the people forget, and therefore does not dwell upon it at sufficient length even to let us know on which side he fought. He says he was present at a siege which, from the general date, must have been that of Leicester; but even this does not help us to ascertain his politics, for that town was besieged by Royalists and Parliamentarians in succession in the course of two or three days. The sympathies of the people went with the Parliamentary troops, chiefly on account of their better treatment of them, for, as Clarendon confesses, " the one side seemed to fight for Monarchy with the weapons of confusion, and the other to destroy the king and government with all the principles and regularity of Monarchy." (B. VII.) If we add to this that Bedfordshire was one of the first counties to declare against the king, we can scarcely doubt that Bunyan was in the service of the Parliament. He was in all probability present at Naseby, and took part in the battle which determined the result of the civil war, for the second siege of Leicester occurred a day or two after that event. It was then that the incident happened which led him to refer to his military experience. "When I was a soldier I, with others, was drawn out to go to such a place to besiege it; but when I was just ready to go one of the company desired to go in my room, to which, when I had consented, he took my place, and coming to the siege, as he stood sentinel, he was shot into the head with a musket bullet and died." That narrow escape impressed him afterwards more than it did at the time, and he returned home after his discharge with a store of warlike imagery to be afterwards used to good purpose, but with no improvement in his character, which he paints in dark colours.

II.

The day, however, began to brighten. It is said that the first circumstance which has a determining influence on a man is the character of his mother, and the next the character of his wife. With respect to the first, he must take what is appointed; but with regard to the second, there is conceded to him a little choice. It was well for Bunyan that he obtained—what no young man should despise—some assistance in this weighty matter. "The few friends he had," says his first biographer, a personal acquaintance, "thought that changing his condition to the married state might reform him, and therefore urged him to it as a seasonable and comfortable advantage; but," continues the good man, " his poverty and irregular course of life made it very difficult for him to get a wife suitable to his inclination." Of course they did; and yet that serious people should interest themselves in him, and that any good young woman should fancy she could reform him, showed that there were, gleaming through his rough exterior, a few sparks of a better nature. Upon such a person as he wanted, notwithstanding his grave disadvantages, "my mercy it was," he says, "to light." The young pair took up house in very sorry plight. "We came together as poor as poor might be, not having so much household stuff as a dish or spoon betwixt us both." But the godly father, who, as you may guess, was not alive when this match was made, had left his daughter a dowry of two books—the "Plain Man's Pathway to Heaven," and the "Practice of Piety." With these instruments, and with the self-forgetful devotedness which you can find in its highest form only in a virtuous woman, she set to work to tame the spirit which had higher destinies than she dreamed of. She did not begin with complaining of his habits, nor treat him to hot words when he came home from his village riots, but beguiled him into the occasional reading of the volumes which she loved for her father's sake, and which she invested with the charm of so many reminiscences of the old man's goodness that John's venerative nature was touched, and he stumbled over the words by the glimmer of his scanty fire, until he recovered his reading, and found "things that were somewhat pleasing." In short, a mighty external reformation soon made its appearance. One thing was given up after another. A sermon from the parson against Sabbath-breaking smote him with terror, and suspended his zeal in that direction for a time; a woman who, though an "ungodly wretch," professed herself shocked by his swearing, made him break off the habit of profanity, which, till that moment, seemed necessary to his existence; dancing and bell-ringing, which he reckoned dangerous from the associations into which they led him, after a year's deliberation, went with the rest; and, to crown all, he took to going to church "twice a-day, and that, too, with the foremost." The neighbours stared, and thought the experiment of domestic life had succeeded to admiration, while the young wife, doubtless, looked on with affectionate pride. Neither she nor her husband then knew the number of roads, some better and cleaner than others, that were found within the City of Destruction, nor saw that a man might walk up and down for a long time in great repute without ever stepping beyond its walls.

III.

The suspicion of this began to visit him. His attempts to keep the divine law did not always succeed, even to his own satisfaction. To-day he thought himself as good as any man in England; to-morrow he broke down and did not know what to make of it. His great mental powers were aroused, and fell upon him, as they had done in his childhood, with terrific fury. Startling dreams affrighted him at night, and thrilling voices penetrated his soul when about his common occupations. Deep as was the horror of great darkness into which these brought him, and terrible as were the thunderings and lightnings that flashed and roared incessantly, nothing could, for a long time, persuade him that the road to heaven did not lie by the way of Sinai at all, but, improbable as it appeared to be, through the "wicket gate." One day, however, as he was working at his trade in the streets of Bedford, soldering and patching the cooking utensils of the poor folk, he came to a door where he saw three or four women sitting in the sun, talking of the things of God. Finding what they were about, and being by this time a "brisk talker" on theology, he went near to them, to find scope for his argumentative abilities. But he presently found himself beyond his depth. They were not disputing at all, but telling each other what had been passing in their minds; with what words and promises they had been refreshed; how they had felt the delights of the love of Jesus, and with what small esteem they regarded their own righteousness. As you see the poor tinker leaning his heavy shoulder upon the wall of the house, hearkening to this sort of discourse, you can fancy his countenance relaxing into an expression of doubt and wonder, as if sounds from some far-off planet had reached his ear. "Methought they spake as if joy did make them speak; they spake with such pleasantness of Scripture language, and with such appearance of grace in all they said, that they were to me as if they had found a new world—as if they were 'people that dwelt alone and were not to be reckoned among their neighbours.'" Bunyan had met with many "brisk talkers" like himself, who were all, in some degree, necessary to his education, and have been immortalised in his works; but none ever equalled these three or four godly women for the enlightenment of his understanding. He returned that day to his work, but their words went with him, and wrought so much upon his heart that he found means of straying again and again into their society. "In fact," says he, "I could not stay away, and the more I went, the more I did question my condition." These deep thoughts he kept secret for a long time. He went through storms of temptation, and narrowly escaped some moral snares, until, when a couple of years had passed, he told his condition to these same "poor people at Bedford." So long as John was an auditor the good women could carry on their talk for his edification, but when he put before them the case of his conscience, and told them what "business" he had been "doing on the mighty waters," in a way which he alone, of most men the world has ever seen, could do, one is not surprised that they should have felt themselves a little nonplussed. They therefore thought it prudent to tell their minister about him, for they were members of the Baptist church that had Mr. Gifford for its pastor.

IV.

Gifford was himself a notable man, and deserves a word in passing. He had been a major in the King's army. Having fallen into the hands of the opposite party, he was imprisoned and condemned to die. On the night preceding his intended execution his sister found her way to his cell, and having perceived the guard to be fast asleep, and his fellow prisoners "dead drunk," she urged him to escape. Gifford glided past the sentinels, got into the fields, and for about three days lay in a ditch, till the search was over. He then travelled to London, which was too public to be safe, and afterwards appeared at Bedford in the character of a doctor. He was a man of education, but a desperate profligate. He hated the Puritans with such intensity that he formed a purpose to kill Harrington, one of their leaders at Bedford, merely for his religious principles. For a heart diseased as his, "there was," as Dr. Southey well remarks, "but one cure." By God's mercy it was administered, and a new life entered into him. He sought the company of the Bedford Puritans, but they were so distrustful of his professions that a long time elapsed before eleven persons—Harrington, whom he meant to kill, being one of them—invited him to become their minister. They had no reason to repent their choice. Bunyan, who afterwards depicted him under the name of "Evangelist," speaks with gratitude of his ministry. He says his teaching was as seasonable to his soul as the "early and the latter rain." It may be permitted us, at the same time, to question whether the mode of acquiring settlement in the truth recommended by him, and probably suggested by his own experience, had not much to do with the length of Bunyan's subsequent conflicts. Great importance was attached to sudden impressions, direct gleams of light, "touches" of isolated words and phrases, and truths which would "bolt" into the mind without any apparent cause. What the untrained strength of his genius needed was a calm and orderly exhibition of evangelical truth, as it is addressed in the Scriptures to the understanding, and through that medium applied to the heart by the Holy Ghost.

V.

But it was permitted for profounder reasons than could have been elicited by human wisdom that he should be precipitated into the depths of agony. "Doleful voices and rushings to and fro" surrounded and assaulted him to an extent unparalleled in his previous experience. It is with deeper significance than strikes most readers of his allegory that he says of the pilgrim, "I heard him here sigh bitterly, for . . . the pathway was here so dark that ofttimes when he lifted up his foot to set forward he knew not where or upon what he should set it next." The Bible, which he searched perpetually, instead of bringing him comfort, added to his tortures. Every threatening seemed levelled at *him*. Not only did Esau and Judas rise up before him, shouting "Our fate shall be yours," but says he, "Methought I should see as if Peter, and Paul, and John, and all the writers did look with scorn upon me and hold me in derision." "One sentence of Scripture did more afflict and terrify me than an army of forty thousand men that might come against me." "These were things," he says finely, "that cared not for Christian's sword, as did Apollyon before, so that he was forced to put up his sword and betake himself to another weapon called *All-Prayer*, so he cried in my hearing, 'O Lord, I beseech Thee, deliver my soul.'" Well might he represent that valley as miles in length, for in his case it required years to travel, with only momentary pauses to prepare for new conflicts. "Nothing now for two years together would abide with me but damnation and an expectation of damnation. I say nothing now would abide with me but this, save some few moments for relief." So fearful and prolonged was the battle that one cannot wonder that his health should suffer. The brain violently exercised acted upon the other great vital organs. His breast-bone seemed to him broken, and "I was suddenly and violently seized with much weakness in my outward man, insomuch that I thought I could not live." Body and mind closed in deadly strife. "Live," cried he, "I must not—die I dare not."

I do not know that any other such history of the struggles of so great a soul has met the eye of the world save that of him who was found, after sore spirit-battles, senseless upon the floor of his cell in the monastery at Erfurt. It was through similar seas of terror and blasphemy that the great German Reformer ploughed his way; and few incidents are more remarkable than the meeting in mid-ocean, and at the height of the tempest, of those two mighty and chastened spirits! Who of the sons of men was better fitted, though at a distance of a century and a half, to shout a passing cheer to Bunyan than Martin Luther? Yet that came to pass. "I did greatly long," said the sufferer, "to see some ancient godly man's experience who had writ some hundreds of years before I was born; for those who had writ in our days I thought (but I desire them now to pardon me) that they had writ only that which *others* felt, or else had, through the strength of their wits and parts, studied to answer such objections as they perceived others were perplexed with, without going down themselves into the deep. Well, after many such longings in my mind, the God in whose hand are all our days and ways, did cast into my hand one day a book of Martin Luther's. It was his comment on the Galatians; it was also so old that it was ready to fall piece from piece if I did but turn it over. Now I was pleased much that such an old book had fallen into my hands, the which, when I had but a little way perused, I found my condition, in his experience, so largely and profoundly handled as if *his* book were written out of *my* heart. This made me marvel, for thus thought I—this man could not know anything of the state of Christians now, but must needs write and speak the experience of former days." " Of particulars here I intend nothing, only this methinks I must let fall before all men : I do prefer this book of Martin Luther upon the Galatians, excepting the Holy Bible, before all the books that ever I have seen, as most fit for a wounded conscience."

VI.

Bunyan's life at this time was spent in travelling about the country in his work, having no settled dwelling-place, but throwing down his weary limbs in any good man's barn when the sun had set, and getting up to his book as soon as the morning streamed its level rays through the cracks of the wall, or above and below the rude door. You can see him going forth to some quiet spot in the fresh air, and sitting down with the Bible on his knees, and Luther in the old tome lying by his side till his turn come to help his brother in distress. "When Christian had travelled in this disconsolate condition some considerable time," runs the fine vein of poetry, in which he seems to allude to it, "he thought he heard the voice of a man, as going before him, saying, 'Though I walk through the valley of the shadow of death I will fear none ill, for Thou art with me.' Then was he glad, and that for these reasons—first, because he gathered from thence that some who feared God was in this valley as well as himself; secondly, for that he perceived God was with them though in that dark and dismal state, and why not, thought he, with me, though by reason of the impediment that attends this place I cannot perceive it ; and thirdly, for that he hoped, could he overtake them, to have company by-and-by . . and by-and-by the day broke; and then said Christian, 'He hath turned the shadow into the morning.'"

After this our friend seems gradually, although not without occasional gratings, to have been floated off the rocks of the law of Moses, and fairly launched upon the ocean of the grace that is in Jesus Christ. It was indispensable to his due preparation for the work which lay before him (although, happily, it is not necessary for every man) to be led through this long succession of sorrows. By those means he acquired that variety of experience, that vividness of conception, that profound sympathy with the Bible, and that mastery of direct and idiomatic phraseology which gave such force to his preaching, and render vital every line of the immortal allegory. Upon some minds the effect of strong religious conflict is to produce an egotistic and malign fanaticism which cares for men only as tools to promote the purposes of ambition—such men have headed sects from Mahomedanism down to Mormonism—but in divinely-instructed spirits, like that of Bunyan, it has served to produce the most touching lowliness, and a certain indescribable delicacy of tenderness towards the burdened and the sorrowful. To whatever extent the chief enemy of the human soul persecuted him—and who can question that he availed himself with heartless cruelty of the imaginative temperament, and the distracted nerves, and the uninformed understanding? —he singularly defeated his own object; for not only did he lose his victim, but qualified him, as he who fights with a skilful enemy acquires the wisdom of his foe, for carrying on the war against his kingdom with rare power and perseverance. On taking leave of this part of his life we may fancy him using the words which he puts into the mouth of "Valiant," and which, it has been, perhaps justly, remarked, would make a lyrical gem even in the pages of Shakespeare:—

"Who would true valour see,
   Let him come hither;
One here will constant be,
   Come wind, come weather.
There's no discouragement
Shall make him once relent
His first avow'd intent
   To be a pilgrim.

"Whoso beset him round
   With dismal stories,
Do but themselves confound;
   His strength the more is.
No lion can him fright,
He'll with a giant fight,
But he will have a right
   To be a pilgrim.

> "Hobgoblin nor foul fiend,
>   Can daunt his spirit;
> He knows he at the end
>   Shall life inherit.
> Then, fancies, fly away;
> He'll not fear what men say;
> He'll labour night and day
>   To be a pilgrim."

VII.

The only allusion we have hitherto made to the public events which were occurring contemporaneously with these spiritual conflicts was occasioned by our hero's short connection with the army. That was in 1645. Four years afterwards Charles was beheaded, and from that moment became terrible. The nation, which had been sickened by his dissimulation, and excited to madness by his tyranny, now throbbed with pity and remorse at the sight of his scaffold. He met death with unquestionable dignity; and the execution of a king, under any circumstances, smites the heart of a generous people. The strength of that sentiment complicated Cromwell's difficulties, and dictated the adoption of severer measures than he would otherwise have chosen. It was an unfortunate necessity; for while his ideas of civil liberty were great, his rule was despotic. His principles, in fact, were embarrassed by his policy, and the military measures of the Commonwealth held freedom in check for half an age. It was not until the close of the century had arrived that it began visibly to advance, and we owe it very much to the fact that civil war has since been unknown in England, that the theoretical views of Cromwell have made, and do still make, so great progress amongst us.

The time has surely come when it is possible to speak impartially of the events of those days; and although I know on which side your sympathies lie, I have too great confidence in your good sense not to venture on the expression of my opinion, that in condemning the tyranny which befel Nonconformists under the Monarchy, we have been in danger of forgetting the intolerance which prevailed during the period of the Commonwealth. There are some systems of which bigotry is a necessary part, and there are others to which it adheres only for a season; but it would have been miraculous if, in a period of intense excitement, and before the province of the civil power had been defined, men holding any system had acted with undeviating charity. It is impossible to forget that the Parliament which had opposed the tyranny of Charles enjoined the "Solemn League and Covenant," an engagement which, had it been proposed by the State for even voluntary adoption, would have been open to great objection, but when enforced on all classes as the pledge of loyalty, presented one of the most intolerant instruments ever wielded. It was defended on the ground of the necessity of securing political unity, but why not for that purpose apply a political test? The Government having established its supremacy was entitled to require submission, particularly on the part of its own officers in Church and State, but to demand for that end adhesion to a religious creed was to insult truth and to violate the rights of conscience. By the unrelenting application of that oath, the Government committed itself to a contest with some of the noblest spirits, for several thousands of the clergy, with a decision which it is impossible not to admire, and which ought not to be forgotten, suffered ejection from their livings rather than submit to it. When Cromwell came to the Protectorate, he sought to moderate the fiery elements around him, but so intimately blended had religion and politics become, and so indispensable was it to the security of a position which had been gained by the sword to use forcible means of repression, that he resorted to laws, in comparison with which even the Covenant was liberal, and which certainly were in diametrical opposition to his speculative opinions. He issued an order which took effect on January 1, 1656, requiring that no ejected Episcopal minister should live as chaplain in any family; preach the Gospel in any place, public or private; administer the sacraments; solemnise marriage, or use the Book of Common Prayer; and that no schoolmaster who had been sequestrated should be retained in any family as teacher, or be allowed to keep any school, public or private. Archbishop Usher waited on him to entreat the withdrawal of this injunction, that the Episcopalians might have the same liberty as other Protestants, but though he at first seemed disposed to comply, he afterwards finally refused.

If this were a lecture on Cromwell it would have been proper to have shown the strong temptations under which he lay to make such an enactment; with what extreme leniency it was enforced, and how correctly, as well as honestly, it was confessed by Bishop Kennet, that "the prejudice he had to the Episcopal party was more from their being Royalists than from their being of the good old Church;" but my purpose is limited to the point of indicating, as common fairness seemed to demand, one of the causes which, during the next reign, brought down a storm of reactionary persecution. That storm was, in fact, stored in the political firmament before the second Charles became visible from the cliffs of Dover. The drops began to fall before he reached the steps of the throne; and immediately afterwards it came down in such torrents as had seldom drenched our soil before. The Commons decreed that the Solemn League and Covenant should be burned by the hangman, and that every member of the House, on pain of instant expulsion, should take the Holy Sacrament after the fashion of the Episcopal Church. Episcopal ordination and the reception by assent and consent of everything contained in the Book of Common Prayer were made imperative on all holders of benefices, and then the glory of the ministry—the conservative power of the nation—walked forth to penury and exile, unattended by circumstances which had softened the parallel scene under the Commonwealth. The King, notwithstanding his vows to the Presbyterians, who thought they had secured him, and his respect for Popery, which he loved with as much sincerity as his nature would admit of, passed Acts which made both these parties droop their plumage. It was made a crime to attend any Dissenting place of worship. A justice might commit, for such an offence, without a jury. For the third breach of the law, sentence of transportation for seven years might be passed, and should the criminal return before that time he might suffer death. The ministers who had been ejected, as well as others who refused the test, were prohibited from coming within five miles of a corporate town, or of any place where they had formerly resided. These, and similar laws, were enforced with the uttermost rigour, for the bishops having been brought up from their dioceses to their old places in the House of Lords, testified their gratitude by preaching without intermission on the Divine right of kings to govern as they chose, and by inspiring the whole body of the clergy with a consuming zeal against Puritanism in all its forms. "For a time," says an eminent historian, "the clergy made war on schism with so much vigour, that they had no leisure to make war on vice. The ribaldry of Etherege and Wycherly was, in the presence and under the sanction of the head of the Church, publicly recited by female lips in female ears, while the author of the 'Pilgrim's Progress' languished in a dungeon for the crime of preaching the Gospel to the poor."—(Macaulay, vol. I., c. 2.)

VIII.

This allusion recalls our subject. Soon after his acquaintance with Gifford, Bunyan was baptized, I suppose in the "lilied Ouse," and united to the church under that good man's care. He was then twenty-five years old, and an object of much interest as a marked monument of Divine grace. It was soon perceived that he had a mind to work, and he was accordingly encouraged to take in hand to speak a word of exhortation. With much weakness and infirmity, he says, he occasionally did so, in the most private manner possible; until the church called him forth to "a more ordinary and public preaching of the Word." He then went about the villages declaring eternal life with all the freshness of a prisoner just released from bondage, for about five years. The proclamation against Dissenters had not then been issued. The formal clergy, however, of more than one sect, had long been annoyed by the power he exercised over the common people. Before Oliver was in his grave they had instituted proceedings against him, which had failed, and now they lost no time in renewing the attempt under happier auspices. In November, 1660, he went to preach in the village of Samsell. He was already sensible of the necessity of proceeding with caution, and generally assembled only a few of the villagers on the premises of some friendly neighbour—places which entwined themselves with the tenderest chords of recollection. "Have you forgot," he touchingly asked, many years afterwards, "the close, the milkhouse, the stable, the barn, and the like, where God did visit your souls?" On this occasion about forty had met, and the preacher had given out the text—" Dost thou believe on the Son of God?" This did not foretell a very treasonable sermon, but a demand for entrance startled the congregation. The door was opened. A justice of the peace and a posse of constables made their appearance. Bunyan was advised to slip out at a back door and escape through a neighbouring wood; but he chose to stand his ground. The magistrate desired him to come down from his place. John informed him that, since he was about his Master's business, he would, for the present, remain where he was. A constable was ordered to fetch him down. He seized him by the coat for that purpose, but Bunyan, with the Bible open in his hand, fixed his eyes upon him; when he turned pale, let go his hold, and stood back. Forgetting the paralysing force of his own look, which all his contemporaries say was very striking—for he was about the middle stature; with ruddy locks; the beard covering the upper lip and decorating the lower; a forehead of ample room, and eyes lighted up by imagination and the memories of spiritual conflict, which looked down into other men's souls —forgetting this, "See," said he, "how this man trembles at the Word of God!" He was, however, summoned in the King's name to surrender, and knowing it was useless to resist, he came down, and with a few parting words to the people, went to the house of the justice. Sureties offered themselves for his appearance at the quarter sessions, but they were not accepted, because he declared that he should reckon it his duty to preach the Gospel as soon as he was set free. He was therefore marched to prison, and the bolts turned upon him. The indictment eventually preferred was as follows:—"That John Bunyan, of the town of Bedford, labourer, hath devilishly and perniciously abstained from coming to church to hear Divine service, and is a common upholder of several unlawful meetings and conventicles, to the great disturbance and distraction of the good subjects of this kingdom, contrary to the laws of our Sovereign Lord the King." To this he was requested to plead guilty or not guilty. He answered thus —" We have had many meetings together to pray to God, and to exhort one another, and we have had the sweet comforting presence of the Lord among us for our encouragement

—blessed be His name therefor. I confess myself guilty no otherwise." No witnesses were examined, but a plea of "guilty" was recorded. His sentence was in these words: "You must be had back again to prison, and be there for three months following; at the three months' end, if you do not submit, and go to church to hear Divine service, and leave your preaching, you must be banished the realm; and if after such a day as shall be appointed you to be gone you shall be found in this realm, you shall stretch by the neck for it." We are at a loss to know whether astonishment or indignation has the predominance in our breasts, when we contemplate such an act. Grateful and glad we are that our civil institutions do now restrain intolerance from such a consummation!

It might not, however, be without service to all whose views of an authoritative ministry are obscure, whether Conformists or Nonconformists, to come out and sun themselves in the noontide of Bunyan's sense. His imprisonment turned very much upon that point. On the morning just mentioned, as he was waiting in the justices' room for his mittimus, "in comes," says he, "an old enemy of the truth, Dr. Lindale, who fell to taunting me in very reviling terms." After a shower of these missiles, Bunyan answered that he had not come there to talk to him but to the Justice, yet if he was minded he could answer any reasonable question. Thus encouraged, he put what he deemed the unanswerable interrogatory, how he could "prove it lawful for him to preach?" John, resorting to his credentials, instantly produced the First Epistle of Peter, fourth chapter, and tenth verse, and read as follows: "As every man hath received the gift, even so minister the same, one to another, as good stewards of the manifold grace of God." "Ay," said his catechiser, "to whom is that spoken?" "To whom?" responded the better theologian, "why, 'to every man that hath received the gift.'" "Indeed," said the doctor (who does seem to have dipped into the New Testament), "I do remember to have read of one Alexander, a coppersmith—('aiming 'tis like at me,' says Bunyan, 'for I was a tinker')—who did much oppose and disturb the apostles." Our friend had more than one battle to fight for the validity of his orders, for the Justice thought fit to attack him when he came before him at the sessions. "Let me a little open that Scripture to you," said the worthy magistrate, after the prisoner had adduced it. "'As every man hath received the gift!' that is, as every one hath received a trade, so let him follow it. If any man hath received a gift of *tinkering*, as thou hast done, let him follow his *tinkering*, and so other men their trades, and the divine his calling." Bunyan could have no objection to Justice Keeling preaching; but he was disposed to question his "hermeneutics." "'Nay, sir,' said I; 'but it is most clear that the apostle speaks here of preaching the Word; if you do but compare both the verses together, the next verse explains this gift—what is it?—saying, 'If any man speak, let him speak as the oracles of God,' so that it is plain that the Holy Spirit doth not so much in this place exhort to civil callings, as to the exercising of those gifts that we have received from God. I would have gone on, but he would not give me leave." It was a discreet decision. After he had been several months in gaol they sent the Clerk of the Peace to argue with him, and he took up another point of attack upon the persecuted text. Cobb was this worthy's name, and he put the case with great shrewdness, after this fashion: "But how shall we know that *you* have received the gift? will you be willing that two indifferent persons shall determine the case, and will you stand by their judgment?"

Bunyan: "Are they infallible?"

Cobb: "No."

"Then," said I, "it is possible my judgment may be as good as theirs; but I will pass by [both parties], and in this case be judged by the Scripture—I am sure that is infallible, and cannot err." "But are you willing," said he, "to stand to the judgment of the Church?" "Yes, sir," said I, "to the approbation of the Church of God; the Church's judgment is best expressed in Scripture." Mr. Cobb, perhaps, did not know that Bunyan had just touched the foundation-stone of Protestantism, but he saw he was immovable, and left the prison, expressing the hope, in which the gaoler seems to have joined, that his obstinacy might not lead to his being sent "beyond the seas, into Spain or Constantinople, or some other remote part of the world."

It is, of course, possible enough that upon the

ground of these interpretations many persons, unfit for the work of the ministry, may reckon themselves entitled to enter it; but if any man entered it in an apostolical spirit it was John Bunyan. When the people had called him out to open the Scriptures to them, and had set him apart, as the churches of old did in similar cases, by "prayer and fasting," with great fear and trembling at his own weakness, he set upon the work, and even when hundreds travelled from all quarters to listen to his vivid words, and some came to be touched by an apprehension of their sins and of their need of Christ, "I could not believe," said he, "that God should speak by *me* to the heart of any man." It was not the promptings of vanity, but the force of an impulse more than human that bore him on. "I preached what I felt, yea, what I smartingly did feel, even that under which my poor soul did groan and tremble to astonishment; indeed, I have been as one sent to them from the dead. I went myself in chains, to preach to them in chains, and carried that fire in my own conscience which I persuaded them to beware of. When I first went to preach the Word abroad, the doctors and priests of the country did open wide against me; but I was persuaded of this, not to render railing for railing, but to see how many of their carnal professors I could convince of their miserable state by the law, and of the want and worth of Christ. I never cared to meddle with things that were controverted or in dispute among the saints, and especially things of the lowest nature; yet it pleased me much to contend with great earnestness for the word of faith and the remission of sins by the death and sufferings of Jesus." How it was possible, with those documents before him, for Dr. Southey to say that "persons were not admonished in these conventicles to labour for salvation, but to regard with abhorrence that Protestant Church which is essentially part of the constitution of this kingdom," it is difficult to say.

IX.

The prisons of England were very different places then to what they are in the present day; and that at Bedford is admitted to have been one of the worst. It was the horrid condition of this place which first rivetted the attention of the immortal Howard—another bright name on the roll of Nonconformity and in the annals of Bedford. In his work on lazarettos and prisons, published in 1789, he fixes upon it one of those rugged notes which owe their force to something sterner than fine composition: "The men and women felons associate together, their night-rooms are two dungeons; only one court for debtors and felons; no infirmary; no bath." Not less characteristic, and even more laconic, is Bunyan's own note, "As I walked through the wilderness of this world I lighted on a certain place where was a DEN!" With no room for air or exercise; with little space for even changing his position; with hardly a chink for seeing the face of nature, and with, at one time, as many as sixty fellow Dissenters, crammed into a space which could not, with common convenience, hold more than twenty—to a man in the thirty-third year of his age, of strong physical constitution, accustomed to great activity, and permitted to pour out his soul in moving appeals and invitations all round the country, such an incarceration, viewed even on the lowest grounds, was no trifling infliction. He had, it is true, what the oppressor can never take away—a clear conscience and a manly spirit. He carried with him his Bible, the prime nourisher both of his intellect and of his immortal hopes, "into which," he says, "I never had so great inlet as now"—

> "For though men keep my outward man
> Within their locks and bars,
> Yet, by the faith of Christ, I can
> Mount higher than the stars."

There were times, however, when the hero subsided into the man, and you will not complain if I let him describe the fact in his own touching words:—"Notwithstanding these helps, I found myself a man encompassed with infirmities. The parting with my wife and poor children hath often been to me in this place as the pulling the flesh from the bones; and then not only because I am somewhat too fond of those great mercies, but also because I should have often brought to my mind the many hardships, miseries, and wants, that my poor family were like to meet with, especially my poor *blind child*, who lay nearer my heart than all I had beside. The thoughts of the hardships I thought my *blind one* might go under would break my heart to pieces. Poor child, thought I, what sorrow art thou like to have for thy portion in this world! Thou must be beaten, must beg, suffer hunger, cold, nakedness, and a thousand calamities, though I cannot now endure the wind should blow upon thee. But yet, recalling myself, thought I, I must venture you all with God, though it goeth to the quick to leave you."

Bunyan alludes in this passage not to the wife who had been a blessing to him when he was little more than nineteen years of age, but to another, worthy to be a successor of the first, whom he had lately married. We could have pardoned a little more talk about both of these excellent women, but with all his communicativeness, he preserves a modest silence on affairs which were purely domestic, and could not benefit his reader. Elizabeth's mind was so affected when her husband, so soon after their marriage, was thrown into prison, that she was ill, nigh unto death, and immediately on her recovery set to work with great energy to seek his enlargement. At the King's coronation there was to be a release of prisoners if they sued out their pardon within a twelvemonth. She first travelled to London, and, finding out Lord Barkwood, presented a petition to him. His Lordship gave her a civil answer, to the effect that the matter rested with the judges of assize. One of those judges was a man of proverbial integrity, who commanded the respect both of Cromwell and of Charles, and whose personal piety qualified him to understand better than most men in his position at that day the grievances under which the Nonconformists were suffering—I mean Sir Matthew Hale. Baxter, in a very interesting passage, tells us that when he resided near Hale, he was often permitted to hold his meetings, though contrary to the letter of the law, with the perfect knowledge of the judge.* His natural reserve, as well as the unmoved

---

* "He was a man of no quick utterance, but spake with great reason. He was most precisely just; insomuch that I believe he would have lost all he had in the world rather than do an unjust act. I, who heard and read his serious expressions of the concernments of eternity, and saw his love to all good men, and the blamelessness of his life, thought better of his piety than of my own. When the people crowded in and out of my house to hear, he openly showed me so great respect before

exterior which befitted his office, doubtless kept secret from Elizabeth Bunyan the depth of sympathy for her which he really cherished. Her first petition he received "mildly," telling her he would do what he could. A second she presented to him while he sat upon the bench. He was going to say something, when Judge Chester stepped up, and said Bunyan was "a hot-spirited fellow, and had been convicted in the court;" on which the experiment fell through.

But Elizabeth was nothing daunted. There was a public room in the town, called the "Swan Chamber," having two large windows opening upon the river, and commanding a view of the bridge prison. There, on one occasion, the judges, many justices, and gentry of the country were assembled. With great trembling she ventured in among them, and presenting herself before Hale, said she had made bold to come again to his Lordship, to know what could be done with her husband. Chester, Twisden, and the justices, each in his turn, and sometimes all of them together, interrupted and badgered her in such a style as makes the self-possession of her answers quite remarkable. Their great argument was that he had pleaded guilty, and was lawfully convicted. When this was denied, Judge Chester bawled out,

"My lord, he is a pestilent fellow; there is not such a fellow in the country again."

Twisden then struck in and demanded, "What! will your husband leave preaching? If he will do so, then send for him."

"My lord," said Elizabeth, with her husband's soul, "he *dares* not leave preaching as long as he can speak."

"See here," said Twisden, "what should we talk any more about such a fellow; must he do what he lists? he is a breaker of the peace."

Elizabeth's answer, that her husband was willing to work at his trade to support his family of four small children, if they would only let him do so, moved the heart of

---

them at the door, and never spake a word against it, as was no small encouragement to the common people to go on; though the other sort muttered [murmured] that a judge should seem so far to countenance that which they took to be against the law."—*Orme's Life of Richard Baxter*, pp. 274, 5.

Hale, and he said, "very mildly," that since they had taken what her husband said as equal to a confession of guilt, she must either apply direct to the King, or get a writ of error.

When Chester heard the advice he was very much offended, and cried, "My lord, he will preach and do what he lists." To which Elizabeth calmly responded, "He preacheth nothing but the Word of God."

"*He* preach the Word of God," said Twisden, as if he was going to strike her, "he runneth up and down and doth harm." "No, my lord," said she, keeping the order of the court, and addressing herself still to Hale, "it is not so; God hath owned him and done much good by him."

"God!" said he; "his doctrine is the doctrine of the devil."

"My lord," said she, sublimely, "when the righteous Judge shall appear it will be known that his doctrine is not the doctrine of the devil."

"My lord," said Twisden to Hale, for he could stand no more, "do not mind her, but send her away!" Sir Matthew did so in a few of his "mild" words, for his heart was one with his petitioner then, as his spirit is now around the throne of God; and Elizabeth took her leave with a dignity to which the matrons of Rome and Sparta never attained. What, indeed, but Christianity can produce a spirit so noble and benevolent as this?—"Though I was somewhat timorous at my first entrance into the chamber, yet, before I went out, I could not but break forth into tears—not so much because they were so hard-hearted against me and my husband, but to think what a sad account such poor creatures will have to give at the coming of the Lord, when they shall there answer for all things whatsoever they have done in the body, whether it be good or whether it be bad."

X.

Under cover of all these apparently hostile events, the purposes of God were advancing to their maturity. Bunyan was to remain in his "den." For six years, it is said, he never crossed its miserable threshold. His intercourse with the external world, almost limited to the daily visits of his wife and children, whom he laboured with his hands to sup port, and with his courage and faith to comfort; exercising his ministry only in occasional messages to the Church, and in expounding the Scriptures to his fellow-prisoners; enriching his fancy with the few glimpses of river and sky, which his grated window permitted; or dwelling with the fond eye of genius on the spider which wove her tissue upon the bars, and the swallow that darted in exulting freedom across the surface of the stream—a tone of tranquillity stole across his nature favourable to that calm activity of the imagination; to the delineation on the soul of that full and defined image of religious truth, and to the going forth of that tender and large charity to men, which were indispensable to the work to which he now unconsciously advanced.

There is an interesting difference discernible in the manner in which the Epic Poem and the Christian Allegory of that age were approached. Milton moved towards his enterprise with deliberate intention. He "smelled the battle," like the war-horse, "afar off." Referring to the period when he was yet a youth in Italy, he says, loftily, "I began . . . to assent . . . to an inward prompting which now grew daily upon me, that by labour and intense study (which I take to be my portion in this life), joined with the strong propensity of nature, I might perhaps leave something so written to after times as they should not willingly let it die." Through thirty years he steadily maintained that purpose, and then in blind old age formed the vast stores of his intellect into creations which the world now could not, if it would, "let die." Bunyan, on the other hand, like the Hebrew bards, when under the influence of the Supreme Spirit, seized the harp without definite purpose; and when the music had quelled his soul into deep stillness his lips opened and poured forth their melody, as much to his own wonder as to that of the world:—

> "I did not understand
> That I at all should make a little book,
> In such a mode; nay, I had undertook
> To make another; which when almost done,
> *Before I was aware*, I this begun."

It is remarkable, too, that while he was not slow to exhibit many of his compositions to his companions—entertaining them with a riddle in verse, a few lines of consolation, or a treatise on some Scriptural topic—he kept secret the lay of the pilgrim, as if there were something singular and sacred in it: as if it came from a higher region than his other thoughts, and was destined, peradventure, to a wider auditory. It was not until it was quite finished, that he ventured to read it aloud;

"Nor was it to any mortal known
Till I had done it."

When we think of the little knot of Nonconformists in that dreary den, gathered about their brother to hear the tale which so many generations in so many climes and languages have since that day pondered—when we fancy them sitting in all directions and in all postures about a place which was never meant to accommodate such a company—when we see the tears and smiles chasing each other across faces reflecting souls which knew how to suffer for Christ—while the seer himself stands near the window, holding up his rude manuscript to the light, and giving it out as it has never been given since, we are ready to say, as "Christian" did on another occasion, "which, when I had seen, I wished myself among them!"

That the scene of this meeting, supposing it to have occurred in Bunyan's apartment, was actually in the gaol, and not as some have conjectured in the house of the gaoler, I have interesting testimony in a letter from my late highly-esteemed friend, William Brodie Gurney, Esq., of Denmark Hill. "There is no doubt," he remarks, "that in consequence of his estimable character the keeper showed him indulgences when he dared to do so, and that there were times at which he was permitted to leave the prison and visit his family, but he was, in company with others, generally imprisoned in a room" (too comfortable a word) "in the gaol; and when my father was in Bedford, as a youth, his grandfather showed him the window of that room, which was situated over the gateway."

But how came this gentleman, the great grandfather of my correspondent, to be a credible witness to that point? He was the personal friend and son-in-law of one of the Nonconformists incarcerated in that place at the same time with Bunyan. We are thus introduced to one of the very individuals of the little captive group. "Mr. Marsom frequently stated to his family that when Bunyan had finished the manuscript of the first part of the 'Pilgrim's Progress,' he read it to his fellow-prisoners with a view of obtaining their opinion as to its publication. The singular descriptions of some of the characters introduced, very much disturbed the gravity of his auditors, and at the first reading some of them doubted the propriety of printing it.

> 'Some said "John, print it," others said "not so."
> Some said "it *might* do good;" others said "no."'

But, on reflection, Mr. Marsom requested permission to take the manuscript into his own cell, to read it quietly alone" —fancy the first reader of the "Pilgrim's Progress"—"and on this perusal he discovered its value, and strongly advised Bunyan to print it."

Brave Thomas Marsom! Is there anything more about him? Yes; a single fact, which I cannot withhold. "I mention it," says Mr. Gurney, "to illustrate the justice of God, and at the same time the Christian spirit of my honoured ancestor. One of the most infamous of the informers often swore that he would lodge Marsom in gaol, even if his legs rotted off in pursuit of him; and he did lodge him in gaol. After the change of times this man was imprisoned in Bedford gaol for some crime, and while in gaol was affected with a complaint, in consequence of which his legs literally rotted. But he whom he had once persecuted, and who had suffered imprisonment through his wicked agency, acting in the spirit of the Saviour, returned him good for evil. Immediately on hearing of his distress he went over to Bedford (he was pastor of a church at Luton), made an arrangement by which a dinner was supplied to him daily, and instead of the straw upon which his diseased body lay, sent him in a bedstead and a mattress, on which he reposed till he died."

It is intimated in this letter that the gaoler was lenient to Bunyan. Such was the fact. For a long time he appears to have been pretty much a prisoner at large. His name occurs repeatedly on the church books as having been present at its meetings; and on one occasion we hear of his having actually visited London. These adventures, however, would have proved disastrous to both ward and keeper had not the guardian angels been more vigilant than the persecutors. That appeared remarkably on the night on which Bunyan, having been permitted to go home, could not sleep, and told his family he must be off to prison. The gaoler was disposed to grumble at being knocked up at so unreasonable an hour; but the secret occasion soon appeared. Early in the morning he was aroused a second time. It was the King's messenger.

"Are all the prisoners safe?"

"Yes."

"Is John Bunyan safe?"

"Yes."

"Let me see him."

There he was! The messenger vanished. When the door was locked again, the gaoler said: "Mr. Bunyan, you may go out whenever you like; for you know better when to return than I can tell you."

He was willing, he says, to stay in prison "until the moss should grow upon his eyebrows," sooner than violate his faith and principles; but the time came when the doors were finally opened with honour to himself. Great obscurity has hitherto rested on the manner of his release. The biographer, whose sketch is preserved in the British Museum, and who appears to have been a friendly Churchman, attributes it mainly to the influence of Bishop Barlow, and nearly all subsequent writers have followed in his train.* Dr. Barlow did not assume the mitre until two years after Bunyan's release, although the old biographer speaks of him as "the then Bishop of Lincoln." This inaccuracy alone indicates partial information; and although Barlow seems to have been a candid and pious man, on terms of intimacy with Dr. Owen, no facts have come to light tending to confirm the honour thus attributed to him.

---

* The Rev. F. Barlow Guy, of Forest School, Walthamstow, wrote to the *Guardian*, after the Bedford Festival, complaining of Dean Stanley's statement that it was Whitehead, the Quaker, who opened for Bunyan the doors of Bedford Gaol. "It is a well-known fact," said Mr. Guy, "that it was through Bishop Barlow's influence that Bunyan's release was obtained." The Dean replied to this, that his version of the story had been settled beyond dispute by recent investigations, in proof of which he referred Mr. Guy to the third volume of Offor. Mr. Guy asserts that he owes a good deal to Bishop Barlow, besides being the possessor of some curious memorials of him. He should show his respect for the Bishop's memory by making himself more familiar than he seems to be with his history.—ED.

The elucidation of the mystery was reserved for the antiquarian zeal of Mr. Offor, who found his way to the State papers, the minutes of the Privy Council, and the records of the Society of Friends, relative to this transaction. From these it distinctly appears that the movement originated with the Quakers. They had suffered more severely than any other sect; and at this juncture nearly five hundred of them were in prison at once. Whitehead, one of their leading men, pressed in spirit by their sufferings, and encouraged by a recent Act of permission to Dissenting worship, wrote to the King, beseeching an interview. He was invited to a meeting of the Privy Council, and, "from the upper end of the council board," pleaded their cause with such effect that the King ended the matter by saying bluntly, "I'll pardon them." He was as good as his word, and ordered the necessary writings to be instantly drawn out. When the other Nonconformists heard of this success, they sought to be included in the same patent, to which the Quakers, forgetting their treatment in controversy at the hands of their brother Dissenters, freely assented. The fees demanded of the prisoners, most of whom had been utterly ruined in their worldly circumstances, arrested them on the threshold.* But when Charles did a chivalrous thing he did it gracefully. On being informed of the circumstance by the indefatigable Whitehead, he commanded that all prisoners should be treated as one man, and be liberated in a body, on the payment of one fee. In this act of general enlargement, which occurred in the month of September, 1672, Bunyan was included. His name may be seen several times repeated in the Magna Charta, preserved in the archives of the Society of Friends, and to them, under Divine mercy, is undoubtedly due the honour of liberating the pilgrim.

XI.

Bunyan lived for sixteen years after his liberation. Although frequently searched for during the recurrence of persecution in the latter part of the reign of Charles, he

---

* Nearly 8,000 persons are said to have suffered death through imprisonment for Nonconformity during this persecution; and from existing documents it appears that there was lost from the same causes about half-a-million sterling—an immense sum to be drawn at that period from the middle and humbler classes.

was never seized; nor was he ever seriously interrupted in that course of extensive usefulness which terminated with his pilgrimage in the memorable year of our Revolution—1688. He had written and published several awakening books while in gaol, and after his release he penned so many more that when even partially collected, some years after his decease, they formed two of those folios which, at that time, were reckoned the most characteristic monuments of our weightiest theologians. Several of these were controversial, for though he never attacked the Quakers again, he was drawn into a prolonged debate with men of the greatest mark in his own denomination. They held the principle, common, I believe, to nearly all religious denominations, that external baptism is a necessary preliminary to participation of the Lord's Supper, while he maintained, as he had been taught by Gifford, and as numberless individuals and some churches now maintain, that Christian character alone, with or without baptism, can be demanded for that purpose. They did not, of course, settle the matter, but the debate brought many incidental advantages, and while it lasted, did not prevent Bunyan's ardent spirit from producing tracts and volumes of universal interest.

It is a most encouraging illustration of the strengthening and purifying power of Christianity that a man of such humble beginning; with no early educational advantages; much worse off than the boys in our ragged schools—although, it must be admitted, of great native talent—should come to write treatises of such force, and imbued with a spirit so great and Scriptural, that one of the most competent judges of our times, the late Dr. Arnold, echoing the sentiments of numbers in the highest places of our literature, said, "I hold John Bunyan to have been a man of incomparably greater genius than any of [our divines], and to have given a far truer and more edifying picture of Christianity."* It may please some literary sentimentalists to style the whole body of our Puritan writers the *Megatheriums* and *mastodons* of a past era, who can be of interest to the present

---

* Dean Stanley's "Life of Arnold," Vol. II., p. 65.

day only as unwieldy curiosities to be stored up in musty receptacles, but it might benefit even them, as it certainly would enrich the soul of every docile student of religious truth, to give some days and nights to the practical treatises of Bunyan. That these compositions, when delivered in the oral form from the pulpit, should have produced a powerful effect, is not surprising. He was not one of those preachers of whom Webster, the American statesman, said that "they take their text from St. Paul, and their sermons from the newspapers;" for all his sentiments are not merely buttressed by verbal quotations from Scripture, but enforced with the very spirit that breathes through the Divine volume, while every sentence seems as if it had been heated in the forge of his own soul. Such things, uttered under the impulse of profound conviction, and with passionate love of souls, would not fail even in our days to repeat the scenes which occurred in his, and respecting which his friend Charles Doe observes, "I have seen by my computation, about 1,200 persons to hear him at morning lecture, on a working day, in dark winter time," and at another place and time, as many as "3,000, so that half were fain to go back again for want of room;" and it could not have been mere tinsel that attracted these crowds, or Dr. Owen would not have replied to the King, when he taunted him with going to hear a "tinker prate": "May it please your Majesty, if I could preach like that tinker, I would willingly part with all my learning."

It cannot however, I presume, be questioned that the work for which this man was especially endowed and educated was the production of that volume which, from its universal reception, the world seems to have been waiting for. The period at which he appeared was rich beyond precedent in writers qualified for the enforcement and defence of religion. There were some of great acquisitions who laid the truths of Christianity on a foundation of evidence; and others who discussed with unsurpassed acuteness the philosophical relations of those truths. There were reasoners who expended their vigour in deducing from Scripture systems of ecclesiastical government; and orators who girded themselves, like strong men for a race, to carry admitted doctrines to the consciences of their auditories. But when the age had studied the "Polity" of Hooker; felt the point of the "Contemplations" of Hall, and been charmed by the ethereal "Commentaries" of Leighton; after it had been humbled by the searching "Expositions" of Owen— elevated by the spirit which breathed through the "Living Temple" of Howe—and at once aroused and comforted in the "Saints' Everlasting Rest" by the vehement appeals of Baxter—something yet remained to be accomplished. There was still demanded a representation of evangelical truth, free from the polemics of the age, and yet such as should do immediate service to the English people; peculiar to no individual, and yet in which men of all times and tongues should feel a personal interest; full of the most momentous truths relative both to experience and to fact, and which yet, by engaging the imagination, should lead captive minds of every intellectual stature, and of all moral complexions. This was a task which could not be entrusted to a man very readily found, even in a period distinguished for its great genius. "Though there were," says Macaulay, "many clever men in England during the latter half of the seventeenth century, there were only two great creative minds." Both of these were on the side of religion. The natural powers of both qualified them to rule in the domain of the imagination. But the providential discipline through which they passed prepared them for works which, though allied, were diverse. "One of those minds produced the 'Paradise Lost.'" Grand, profound, harmonious, resounding through all time, and gaining fit audience in all countries, it was yet far from fulfilling the demand which rose from the heart of the world. It required in its readers some learning: but most men are not learned; it abounded in lofty speculation: but the majority of men are practical; it gave the poetry of redemption: but sinners crave redemption itself. How "the other" was trained—how it was emptied from vessel to vessel, and transferred from one furnace to another—how it was conducted from the abyss of misery to the height of blessedness, and made to hear "words not possible for a man to utter," until the world received from it the "Pilgrim's Progress"—may be seen by searching the life of Bunyan.

For six years after his liberation the author kept the

manuscript in concealment, and it was only because he was unable to obtain a unanimous verdict in its favour from the few to whom he had entrusted its contents, that he resolved to cast "the lot into the lap," and to leave the "disposing thereof unto the Lord." It crept forth, at length, in a small duodecimo of coarse paper: the humble form which suited the convenience of the travelling booksellers and the weight of the poor man's purse. But seldom has any book acquired a more rapid, perhaps not one a more extensive and enduring circulation. Before the second part was issued, which was six years after the appearance of the first, it had been hailed—who can tell with what delight—by those brother pilgrims who had quitted our shores for forced expatriation to the forests of New England; it had delighted the kilted Highlander in the language of the Gaël—kindled the wild eye of the Irish peasant in the tones of the Celtic—and edified the dwellers in Cambrian valleys in the language of Ancient Britain. France had not deemed it too grave to introduce to her liveliest circles; nor Holland too gay to be read by her soberest citizens. Nearly every country of Europe, in marvellously short time, possessed itself of the treasure; and now, since the world has been opened by Christian missions, there is scarcely a spot on which the human race is found where you may not track the steps of "Pilgrim." The Burman reads the story in the round letters of his mother tongue; the Chinese, in the symbol-pictures of his; the degenerate Arab, in the fairy characters by which his fathers expressed some of the finest literature of the world; and, by the ruined walls of Jerusalem, the sad Jew regales his fancy, and feels his heart soften towards Jesus the Nazarene, by perusing it in the square unpointed Hebrew: eldest shrine of celestial allegory, dream, and poem. Travel whither you choose, along the stream of the Ganges—through the rich groves of Ceylon—by the sparkling shores of Polynesia—or under the broad-leaved bananas of New Zealand, you shall meet thousands who rejoice and tremble over the vicissitudes of "Christian." The African chief has thrown aside his spear, joined the group of Christian listeners, and obtained his first glimpse of redeeming love through the veil of the parable; while in Madagascar forests the persecuted flock of God, by pondering it in the manuscript volumes which they had written with their own hands, have fitted their souls for the steel, the poison, the precipice, and the martyr's crown!

When the good man, after having attained to his sixtieth year, and travelled from Reading to London in heavy rain, sought the home of a Christian tradesman on Snow Hill, and spent there ten days in meek suffering and edifying conversation, he breathed forth his redeemed spirit to go to a world in which he was to be better known than he had been in this. Already numbers from his own country were there, presenting songs of thanksgiving to God for blessings received through his pen. As time moved on, men of neighbouring lands, divided below by languages and religions, joined the throng, and with one heart united in the strain. When, at length, the regions which had dwelt in the night of heathenism sent up their tribes—unseen in those realms before—they mingled in the thickening multitude and blended their new voices in the anthem until it rose to the thunder of many waters; and if it continues to be the pleasure of God that every one who translates the Bible into a new tongue shall send out in its train the annals of the Pilgrim, we shall reach, without any extravagance of thought, this instructive conclusion, that, when we have excepted the inspired writers, there will, probably, be no individual of the human family of greater interest to so large a number of the redeemed inhabitants of heaven, than one who, in the name of religion, was condemned for twelve years to a dungeon in Bedford.

The Scenery and Characters of Bunyan.
BY THE REV. J. STOUGHTON, D.D.

Dr. Stoughton said it was by quite an accident that he was there that day; he was not an invited guest, but in a certain sense a self-proffered one. When he heard what was going on at Bedford he was extremely anxious to be present, and as the Dean of Westminster asked him to come, he was invited to this dinner through the kindness of a friend. The Mayor had requested him to give as a toast, "The Memory of John Bunyan." Before doing so he would just say, that when he attended at a dinner not long ago he heard it remarked that an after-dinner speech should not consist of more than twelve sentences. The memory of John Bunyan was, however, a very large subject, yet as they had heard much respecting it he was afraid of treading ground which had been well trodden by those who had preceded him. He wished, however, that they should again do honour to Bunyan's genius. It had been spoken of already, but there was one point he should like to impress upon them, and it was this —that whilst his genius was eminently idealistic, it was equally realistic. The characters in his works were allegorical personifications of vices and virtues, yet people rose from reading his dream with impressions of character as lively as those derived from the perusal of Sir Walter Scott or William Shakespeare. There was this peculiarity in almost all his characters—they were just like people in the Midland counties, like those who lived and walked in the streets of Bedford. Moreover, it had been said that Bunyan had not the power of word-painting: yet he brought before their eyes scenes extraordinarily vivid. He (Dr. Stoughton) had, while sitting in that room, heard conversation with reference to places Bunyan might have had in view; but he must differ from some of his friends who thought Bunyan had in his mind scenes in this neighbourhood. Depend upon it, he had never seen anything corresponding to the Valley of the Shadow of Death. He never saw anything like the Land of Beulah or the Delectable Mountains. And yet in his second dream he referred to the scenery of the first as though the whole were a reality, even as we are in the habit of alluding to localities with which we are familiar from day to day. Next the speaker invited the guests to do honour to Bunyan's character. Bunyan was far removed from the Anglican type of religious life—as far as could be from such a character as George Herbert; he was a Puritan out and out; and the Puritan stamp in his dreams was actually reproduced in his own Christian life and character. He was Christian, Evangelist, and Greatheart all in one; a pilgrim to heaven, a preacher of the Gospel, the leader and guide of a church, acting the part of him who conducted Christiana and her children to the river of death, whence they passed to the gates of the

Golden City. Further, Dr. Stoughton asked those present to do honour to Bunyan as one of the great teachers of religious liberty and comprehension. For instance, he gave practical solution to a difficulty of his day, by extending the boundary of church communion. He would not make adult baptism by immersion a term of communion. In Bunyan's model church there was no difference made between Baptists and Pædo-Baptists. He (Dr. Stoughton) had never lost an opportunity, and he should be sorry to do so now, of expressing his inability to see that it was necessary to have two such denominations. John Bunyan could not, and, if he could not with his marvellous imagination, it was strange indeed that Christians in the present day should still keep up that line of separation. In turning over the papers in the Bodleian Library at Oxford, he had found a document which mentioned certain persons in this borough before the Revolution in the reign of James II. It was to the effect that John Bunyan and another individual named Margetts were prepared to do their utmost to return two members to Parliament who would seek to repeal all penal laws touching religion. That showed what kind of man he was, and the whole of his life went to illustrate principles of freedom, for he was ever a foe to religious intolerance. The speaker rejoiced at this opportunity of speaking in honour of Bunyan. This town might now be regarded as the land of Goshen, and when there were strife and commotion elsewhere they would turn their eyes to Bedford, where Christian charity was manifested by all denominations. He was afraid that his remarks had not proved to be "silvern" speech, but he invited the company to honour the memory of John Bunyan in "golden" silence.

The Secret of Bunyan's Influence.

BY S. WHITBREAD, ESQ., M.P.*

Mr. Mayor, I have to express my sincere thanks for the very kind manner in which the health of the Borough Members has been received by the present company.

---

* Mr. Whitbread is grandson of the celebrated politician whose name he bears. He was first elected for Bedford in 1852. His illustrious grandfather, the friend of Chatham, bequeathed £500 to the church at Bedford, in honour of Bunyan's memory.

During the many years I have known Bedford, I have never seen the town look better, or the people more happy, or more united in the promotion of one object, than to-day. The work of art presented to the town by the Duke of Bedford is a noble one, and the gift has been well appreciated.

It was my good fortune to be amongst those who this afternoon in the Corn Exchange listened with unbounded interest to those admirable essays on the character and writings of Bunyan—essays which I am glad to know are not for us alone, they will be carried to-morrow by the newspapers to the whole country. And as I listened to speaker after speaker endeavouring to account for the marvellous hold which Bunyan's writings had taken upon the world, I was reminded of a passage in "Grace Abounding," that wonderful work describing his soul tossed from joy to doubt, from doubt almost to despair, and anon back again to joy, where Bunyan says that at one time he greatly longed to see the experience of some ancient godly man who had written long before; for of those who wrote in his own day he thought that they wrote only that which others felt without themselves going down into the deep. At that time Martin Luther's comment on the Galatians came into his hands, and he says of it, when he had a little way perused it, "I found my condition in his experience so largely and profoundly handled, as if his book had been written out of my heart."

And that is the story of the influence which Bunyan's works exercise over us. He had penetrated deeply into the human heart, and he spoke his experience frankly.

The outward appearance of this town has so much changed that he would not know it now; our ways and manners have changed too; but the springs of action in the human heart are the same, and it is well that we should have this statue on St. Peter's Green, if for no other reason, that it may remind us that deep down in our hearts are the fires of sectarian hatred, ready, unless we learn to school them well, to break forth in our day as in his.

I hope those present will pardon this short digression. I know that it is not within my commission to speak on this subject; but I could not pass by the monument of this great man without casting my humble tribute there.

The Newspaper Press on the Celebration.

THE PARALYSED DEMON OF INTOLERANCE.

It is but natural that Bunyan should have a statue at Bedford, and the only marvel is that the tribute should have been delayed so long. People are generally eager enough to pay all honour to immortal memories, the more so when they may hope to shine themselves in the reflected lustre. In this case, however, the seeming neglect may be easily explained. In the lustre of Bunyan's famous book, his connection with Bedford had been almost forgotten. It is not his actions that have made his name immortal, but one single work of his. A greater tribute to the memory of the great Dissenter than the inauguration of any number of statues is the fact that a distinguished dignitary of the Church should have been chosen to play the chief part in the ceremony—the more so that the circumstance strikes no one as extraordinary. So far, at least, as Bunyan is personally concerned, he has paralyzed that demon of Old Intolerance—the giant Dean Stanley alluded to as crippled, if not killed. No one now cares to remember whether the author of the most fascinating allegory that ever struck despair into the souls of imitators was a Dissenter.—*The Times.*

BUNYAN'S BEDFORD LIFE.

If Bunyan never had made himself immortal, if he had never proved himself the "Prince of Dreamers," if, in a word, he had never written the "Pilgrim's Progress," Bedford would still have a right to remember and to cherish his name. It was in Bedford that he was "converted," in Bedford that he ministered, in Bedford gaol that he was held for many years under fluctuating conditions of duresse, now like a favoured military prisoner on parole, free to do almost anything, or go almost anywhere he pleased, and now coerced and restricted like the commonest criminal; and it was in Bedford that his preaching and his pastoral organisations acquired such subsequent influence that people called him Bishop Bunyan. Dante is not more closely associated in history with Florence, nor Shakespeare with Stratford, nor Rabelais with Meudon, nor Wordsworth with Rydal, than Bunyan is with Bedford. Art has again and again busied itself with some passage of Bunyan's Bedford life, as he preached in his gaol, as he made his tagged laces there, as he worked there at the opening passages of his immortal allegory. It was only by a chance that Bunyan did not end his career in the town which he has made famous. Great inspirations of genius had before Bunyan's time been first moulded into shape in the atmosphere of a prison. If the story be not true which so long asserted that "Don Quixote" was begun in the gaol of a little town of La Mancha—a story which derives some plausibility, at least, from some words in the book itself—then assuredly the finest work of imagination ever begun within the walls of a prison was begun in Bedford gaol by Bunyan.—*Daily News*.

VANITY FAIR AND THE PILGRIM.

All the world knows why the Tinker of Elstow should receive the posthumous honours of Vanity Fair: all the world has heard of him—all the world's readers read him —be it the pilgrim progressing slowly and tearfully through the snares and mockeries of its booths; be it a Mr. Worldly-Wiseman, who merely loves good writing; be it Faithful, or be it Lord Facing-both-ways—everybody has read John Bunyan's wonderful book. With that one piece of rude but real genius he has carved his own statue and built himself a monument which must be still fresh when the bronzed figure unveiled to-day in Bedford is ancient and time-worn. The roysterers of the Restoration who clapped the glorious Tinker into the bilboes could not, with all their locks and bolts, confine his mind. "Stone walls do not a prison make, nor iron bars a cage." Never did any man justify that proud saying so thoroughly as the writer of the "Pilgrim's Progress." In the flesh he was a prisoner of the English Cavaliers, making three-tagged laces to keep his wife and family in bread, and all those cruel years fed himself on gaol food; but in the spirit he was free along with Christian and Faithful, walking upon that road—imaginary, but so plain—feigned, but so little fictitious—where millions of feet have since followed his, and millions of pilgrims measured every stage and step of the way.—*Daily Telegraph.*

A TORY COUNTERBLAST.

When we talk of the persecution of Bunyan, we should remember that Bunyan and Penn were probably the only Dissenters who would not have requited that persecution tenfold. The King and the Church were dealing with merciless persecutors and unscrupulous murderers; and they only fulfilled the commission given them by the nation in taking care that at any cost the Puritans should be prevented from getting the upper hand again. Bunyan, like other innocent men, suffered for being found in evil company. Dr. Stanley seems to have misread the history of Puritanism, as he certainly has misread the history of the "glorious" Toleration Act. It was in no sense a triumph of liberty or a security for the rights of conscience.—*The Standard.*

THE "PILGRIM'S" CHIEF SERVICE TO MANKIND.

The power of Bunyan's book lies, we are persuaded, somewhere beyond even all its poetical and spiritual beauty. It is—the fact has never been duly noted—the first great work which distinctly sets forth "Progress" as the law of life. It may well be questioned, indeed, if much of the lively and familiar sense of this truth which has been for the last century common amongst us, be not in a great measure due to the story of "Christian" beginning his course of the Wicket Gate, and pressing ever onwards till he reaches the Celestial City at the end of all his labours and perils. St. Paul had set forth the Christian career as a race and a combat, but in the common teaching of Christian divines from that time downwards, the great initial change of "conversion" or "regeneration" had always been placed so prominently forward that the bulk of their followers have taken it for granted, that when it was accomplished heaven was won and there was little more to be done. Bunyan re-wrote the Natural History of the human soul. From Bunyan's time to our own this conception of the inner life has become more clear, and tens of thousands of souls have had to thank him for reading their own story aright and escaping the dread dungeons of Giant Despair, even when they had, like Christian, wandered far from the right way.—*The Echo.*

THE VICTORY OF GENIUS.

There is nothing, or very little, that is new to be said about John Bunyan, or the "Pilgrim's Progress," or Allegory as an art, and yet it is just at this moment so hard to abstain from saying something. The irony of circumstance is so delicious, the victory of genius over prejudice so perfect, the triumph of the writer over the squire and the magistrate—the triumph of the really strong over the apparently strong—so suggestive of hope. In 1674, Bedford imprisoned a travelling tinker for his impudence in preaching what he had to preach, which, as it happened, was a moderated form of Calvinism. In 1874, Bedford raises a statue, given by a Duke, to her greatest citizen, that very travelling tinker who never thought anything, or did anything, or said anything which the world has cared to remember, except writing, amidst the foulnesses and the stenches of her borough gaol, a story embodying the theology he preached. The names of the squires are forgotten, or remembered as the Lucys of Charlecote are remembered, as Lilliputians who imprisoned Gulliver, and whose names have lived for ages because a butcher's man condescended to hold them in contempt; the wretched bourgeois are mould, possibly yielding corn; and the new generation raises a statue to their victim, the "low" tinker. The victory is too perfect, too complete, to pass without one pleasurable word.—*The Spectator.*

BUNYAN AT BEDFORD.

Bunyan the Pilgrim, dreamer, preacher,
Sinner and soldier, tinker and teacher,
For heresy scoffed, scourged, put in prison—
The day of Tolerance yet un-risen—
Who heard from the dark of his dungeon lair
The roar and turmoil of Vanity Fair,
And shadowed Man's pilgrimage forth with passion,
Heroic, in God-guided poet-fashion,

The Want of our Age.

Has now his revenge; he looks down at you
In a ducally-commissioned Statue,—
A right good artist gave life and go to it,
But his name's Boehm, and Rhyme says " no " to it—
And the Dean of Westminster, frank and fluent,
Spoke Broad-Church truths of the Baptist truant.

Punch likes the Duke and he likes the Dean,
And the summer air in the summer green,
When the Anabaptist poet and clown
Was set up as the glory of Bedford town:
But ducal and decanal folk should learn
That to deal with the Past is of small concern;
That light for the day's life is each day's need,
That the Tinker-Teacher has sown his seed;
And we want *our* Bunyan to show the way
Through the Sloughs of Despond that are round us to-day,
Our guide for straggling souls to wait,
And lift the latch of the wicket-gate.

The Churches now debate and wrangle,
Strange doubts theology entangle;
Each sect to the other doth freedom grudge,
Archbishop asks ruling of a judge.
Why comes no pilgrim, with eye of fire,
To tell us where pointeth minster spire,
To show, though critics may sneer and scoff,
The path to "The Land that is very far off"?
The People are weary of vestment vanities,
Of litigation about inanities,
And fain would listen, O Preacher and Peer,
To a voice like that of this Tinker-Seer;
Who guided the Pilgrim up, beyond
The Valley of Death, and the Slough of Despond,
And Doubting Castle, and Giant Despair,
To those Delectable Mountains fair,
And over the River, and in at the Gate
Where for weary Pilgrims the Angels wait!

—Punch.

"THE WHIRLIGIG OF TIME."

Looked at in any aspect the scene was remarkable. That a noble Duke should raise a statue to a "low tinker" is a social triumph; that a literary Dean should pay homage to the genius of an uncultured man shows the fraternity of the world of letters; that the memory and work of a Calvinist preacher should be honoured by representatives of all creeds is a victory of pure religion over sectarianism; but, above all, that a man once imprisoned for daring to preach the Gospel to the poor should have the anniversary of his release kept with public rejoicing in the very town in whose dungeon he was confined is a grand indisputable testimony to the progress of religious liberty. It is altogether very wonderful, and no more noteworthy incident has happened during this last quarter of a century. That statue of John Bunyan marks the spot to which the tide of ecclesiastical intolerance has receded at the present time. We do not forget, and the reflection is tinged with melancholy, that it has taken no less than two hundred years to overcome the bigotry and prejudice of which Justice Keeling was simply the representative and exponent, and that this result has been achieved only by means of a lengthened and painful conflict. The retrospect is not a pleasant one, yet Nonconformists have no need to be ashamed of the part their ancestors took in the struggle. And we cannot forget that the conflict is not yet over. We have to continue the warfare against the last remnants of the old system of intolerance which are existing in society at the present hour. The erection of a statue to John Bunyan is an encouragement to the advocates of religious equality to persevere in their endeavours. Having accomplished so much we need not despair of bringing public opinion completely to our side.—*English Independent*.

THE TRIUMPH OF CHRISTIAN CHARITY.

The church bells were ringing in honour of John Bunyan! All the distinctions with which Englishmen are only too familiar had vanished under what Dr. Chalmers would have called the blessed expulsive force of a generous emotion. Churchman and Dissenter had come together as brethren. The peer and the peasant found common ground in doing honour to the tinker of Elstow. Even the Roman Catholic priest and the Irvingite Apostle had come down from their isolated pedestals, and moved, like ordinary human beings, in the joyous throng. This is Bedford town, where two hundred years ago Bunyan was writing the "Pilgrim's Progress" in his prison cell; but it seems to have grown into something closely akin to the Celestial City. The incidents of such a day are worthy of being held in everlasting remembrance. They marked, in most striking form, the progress of the glorious principles for which Bunyan suffered. Such a triumph of Christian charity was never before seen in England. I call to mind the words of an eloquent Scottish peer, which, heard in childhood, have never been forgotten. At the Burns Festival on the banks of the Doon, held thirty years ago, the Earl of Eglinton declared that "repentant Scotland" had assembled to pay to the dead poet the tribute denied him while he was alive. As I listen at Bedford to the testimonies of the peer and the Church dignitary, I see repentant England recognising the greatness which was condemned to the gaol and the principles which were scorned.—"*An Eye-witness*" *in the Freeman.*

POPISH AND CLERICAL SLANDER AGAINST BUNYAN.

In the week following the Bunyan Festival, the Rev. W. J. Stracey, dating from Buxton Vicarage, Norwich, addressed a letter to the *Guardian*, a Church of England newspaper, in which he revived an old Popish slander, that Bunyan plagiarised the "Pilgrim's Progress" from the "Pylgremage of the Sowle," by Guillaume de Guileville, of which there is a French MS. copy in the British Museum. Mr. Stracey said he had been told that a Miss C—— printed an English translation of this MS. to show that Bunyan's allegory was nearly *verbatim* a copy of De Guileville's, "with a few alterations here and there to give it the tinge of originality." Mr. Stracey, who wrote from mere hearsay, closed his indiscreet epistle with the remark: "I must leave it to others to determine whether the Church or the Nonconformists have the right to claim the original work."

This mendacious charge against Bunyan was first made by a Roman Catholic in the *Freeman's Journal*, September, 1859, and was thoroughly investigated and disproved by Mr. Offor. Two clergymen, of more learning and larger heart than Mr. Stracey, wrote to the *Guardian* to set that gentleman right. These were the Revs. T. A. Carr, of Cranbrook, and C. E. Steward, of St. Peter's, Southampton. In the introduction to the Hansard Knollys Society's edition of the "Pilgrim's Progress" will be found an analysis of "The Pylgremage of the Sowle," drawn from a careful perusal of the original edition by Caxton, compared with the manuscript written in 1413. This analysis leaves no doubt of John Bunyan's originality.

Apropos of Mr. Stracey's letter, the writer of "Table Talk" in the *Guardian* made an interesting note :—

"A letter in our Correspondence last week mentions the 'Pelerinage de l'Ame' of Guy or Guillaume de Guileville as having given Bunyan not only the idea, but even in many places the very words of his allegory. The 'Peleringe' was published in 1858 and 1859 in English, by Miss C. J. Cust; it is not an uncommon book. There are many points of resemblance between it and the 'Pilgrim's Progress,' but they are not greater than might be expected where the subject was almost identical, and the general drift of the teaching the same. There the resemb'ance ceases. The statement that Bunyan made a *verbatim* copy has long been refuted. Guy de Guileville wrote in *French* and in *verse*, though an early prose version is in existence and was among the MSS. recently exhibited at the Burlington Club. Caxton's translation was used by Miss Cust. It is in prose, interspersed with poetry, and a copy of the original may very probably have been seen and read by Bunyan. It will not, however, be very easy to claim the French mediæval monk for our Church, any more than the English tinker of the seventeenth century. It might be easier to claim Caxton, to whom many of the technical terms of later English theology may be traced."

The *Tablet*, Roman Catholic paper, devoted a paragraph to the subject, in which it was asserted that Mr. Stracey had "revealed" the "curious fact" that "beyond his own ignorant interpolations, John Bunyan had nothing to do with the 'Pilgrim's Progress.'"

www.ingramcontent.com/pod-product-compliance
Lightning Source LLC
Chambersburg PA
CBHW022139160426
43197CB00009B/1356